Phrase Fact Finder

Terry O'Brien is an academician by vocation and a passionate quiz enthusiast by avocation. He has written and edited several bestselling books and series, including the Little Red Book series, the Fun Facts series, the Classic Tales for Children series, and the Fables from India series.

PHRASE

FACT

FINDER

TERRY O' BRIEN

RUPA

Published by
Rupa Publications India Pvt. Ltd 2014
7/16, Ansari Road, Daryaganj
New Delhi 110002

Sales Centres:

Allahabad Bengaluru Chennai
Hyderabad Jaipur Kathmandu
Kolkata Mumbai

ISBN: 978-81-291-3537-7

First impression 2014

10 9 8 7 6 5 4 3 2 1

Printed by Thomson Press India Ltd, Faridabad.

INTRODUCTION

Why do we say *raining cats and dogs*? If we bought *a pig in a poke*, would it be a good bargain. Where on earth did these commonly used phrases come from? Were they *born out of nowhere*? This book helps uncover the interesting origins of many common phrases. So come, let us *grasp the nettle*.

In Norse mythology, cats symbolized heavy rain, while dogs were associated with Odin, the storm God, who represented wind—hence the phrase *raining cats and dogs*. If we get cheated when we bring something without scrutinizing it, we have bought a *pig in a poke*. (*Poke* here refers to a bag; during village fairs in England a pig was brought to the market in a poke and sold and one realized the defects of the pig only on returning home and opening the opening the bag!). This book helps uncover surprising connections between words and phrases, their origins and their history.

Useful for reference and fun for browsing, *Phrase Fact Finder* is also an interesting way to expand your vocabulary and learn things about the English language that you never imagined!

A

Above board

Meaning: Legitimate.

Origin: Cardsharps place their hands under the board or table to stack the deck. If they keep their hands above the board, they can be presumed to be performing without trickery.

Absence makes the heart grow fonder

Meaning: The lack of something increases the desire for it.

Origin: The Roman poet Sextus Propertius wrote in Elegies: 'Always toward absent lovers, love's tide stronger flows.'

A cat may look at a king

Meaning: It refers to an impertinent comment made by someone of lower status (i.e. the cat looking) to someone with higher status (i.e. the king).

Origin: Originates from the 16th century, and appeared in a political pamphlet in 1652.

Acid test

Meaning: A sure test, giving an incontestable result.

Origin: The original acid test was developed in the late 18th century and relied on nitric acid's ability to dissolve other metals more readily than gold. To confirm that a find was gold it was given 'the acid test'.

A countenance more in sorrow than in anger

Meaning: A person or thing that is viewed more with sadness than with anger.

Origin: This is from Shakespeare's *Hamlet*, 1602.

A diamond in the rough edges

Meaning: Someone who is basically good-hearted but lacks social graces and respect for the law.

Origin: This refers to the original unpolished state of diamond gemstones, especially those that have the potential to become high quality jewels. It is more commonly expressed in the form of 'rough diamond'. The term is often now used to describe people on the edge of the criminal fraternity who, while they may not commit serious crimes themselves, probably know people who do.

A fish out of water

Meaning: Someone who is in a situation they are unsuited to.

Origin: This metaphor is from Chaucer in *The Canterbury Tales*. *Prologue*: '...a monk, when he is cloister less; Is like to a fish that is waterless.'

A friend in need is a friend indeed

Meaning: Someone who helps you when you are in need is a true friend.

Origin: Quintus Ennius wrote in 3rd century BC: '*Amicu certus in re incerta cernitur*'. This translates from the Latin as 'a sure friend is known when in difficulty'.

A house divided against itself cannot stand

Meaning: Literal meaning (house meaning household).

Origin: From the Bible, *Matthew 12:25*: 'And Jesus knew their thoughts, and said unto them, every kingdom divided against itself is brought to desolation; and every city or house divided against itself shall not stand'.

Alter ego

Meaning: A second self.

Origin: The use of this phrase derives from the Latin 'other I'. This is a psychoanalysis term. The concept of an alter ego, that is, a second self, was put forward by Cicero as a philosophical construct in 1st century BC Rome. The term is also the name of a popular computer game. Recently it has been much used in stories of superheroes like Superman and Batman, who require a day-to-day human guise. It is also found in the story of Dr Jekyll and Mr Hyde.

A load of codswallop

Meaning: Nonsense.

Origin: Hiram Codd, an English soft drinks maker during the 1870s, developed a technique for bottling lemonade. This process involved the insertion of a glass marble as a stopper into the neck of the bottle. When the bottle was shaken the resulting pressure from the fizzy pop forced the marble against the neck to form a seal. The device was called the Codd Bottle. 'Wallop' is a slang term for beer.

An albatross around one's neck

Meaning: A lifelong burden from which there is no escape.

Origin: In *The Rime of the Ancient Mariner*, Samuel Taylor Coleridge tells the story of a sailor whose ship was trapped by ice and who was visited by an albatross. The bird was regarded as a lucky symbol at sea and, sure enough, soon afterwards the vessel was freed from the ice. But then the hapless mariner shot the albatross and almost instantly a curse befell the ship. The furious crew hung the dead bird around the sailor's neck as a punishment, but one by one each of them died, eventually leaving the mariner alone. Then, while watching the beautiful sea snakes in the water around the ship, the mariner began blessing them and the albatross dropped from his neck. The ship was freed once again and the sailor's life had been saved. From then on, the man travelled the earth telling his tale and encouraging love for all God's creatures. The moral of the story is that an albatross is a symbol of personal guilt, and freedom from it must be earned.

An assassin

Meaning: A paid mercenary, prepared to kill another for a fee.

Origin: The original assassins were a group of Muslim fanatics who came together in Persia around 1090. Their leader was one Hasan-e Sabbah who himself died in 1124. For generations they had been directing murderous and violent attacks against their ruling administrations, usually after fuelling themselves with hashish. This is how they became known, and feared, as the Hashashin or 'hashish eaters'.

An eye for an eye, a tooth for a tooth

Meaning: This follows the notion that for every wrong done there should be a compensating measure of justice.

Origin: This is based on the Code of Hammurabi. Hammurabi was King of Babylon, 1792-1750 BC. The code survives today in the Akkadian language. It is also used in the Bible, *Matthew 5:38*: 'Ye have heard that it hath been said, an eye for an eye, and a tooth for a tooth.'

April fool

Meaning: The victim of a trick played on April 1st, or the trick itself.

Origin: March 25th used to be New Year's Day in England; April 1st marked the climax of the New Year's revels, when tricks were played.

A safe pair of hands

Meaning: A reliable, if somewhat dull, person who can be entrusted not to make a mistake with a task.

Origin: Applied to politicians or diplomats who were given sensitive work that required careful handling. Now used in cricket for a good fielder.

ASAP

Meaning: As soon as possible.

Origin: This is an initial that can be pronounced by spelling out the letters a. s. a. p. or as a word.

As dead as a dodo

Meaning: Dead.

Origin: The dodo was a flightless bird somewhat like a turkey. It was native to Mauritius; the last live specimen was seen in 1662 and they are thought to have died out completely by 1690.

As happy as Larry

Meaning: To be very happy.

Origin: Larry is the best known character in the world of similes. The expression he instigated is most likely Australian or New Zealand in origin.

As keen as mustard

Meaning: Very enthusiastic.

Origin: The long-standing enthusiasm for the Sunday roast was real in England. Mustard was an essential accompaniment to beef. It became associated with vigour and enthusiasm because it added zest and flavour.

As old as Methuselah

Meaning: Very old.

Origin: Methuselah was a Hebrew patriarch who was supposed to have lived for 969 years.

At beck and call

Meaning: To be at someone's beck and call is to be entirely subservient to them; to be responsive to their slightest request.

Origin: 'Call' is used here with its usual meaning. 'Beck' is merely a shortened form of 'beckon', which means 'to signal silently, by a nod or motion of the hand or finger, indicating a request or command'.

A bigger bang for your bucks

Meaning: More for your money.

Origin: Generals and political leaders have argued over the costs of the military since time immemorial.

A bird in the hand is worth two in the bush

Meaning: It's better to have a lesser but certain advantage than the possibility of a greater one that may come to nothing.

Origin: In the days of medieval falconry, a bird in the hand (the falcon) was a valuable asset and certainly worth more than two in the bush (the prey).

A battle royal

Meaning: A zealously fought contest, sporting or otherwise. It can be on battlefields, either literal or metaphorical.

Origin: This began with the obsession with cock fighting. It was such a popular pastime that people of every class, even the aristocracy and members of the royal families across Europe would send their prized cocks into the fray. The royal cocks were usually the most magnificent of all and consequently often the best of the fighting birds.

A bean feast

Meaning: A company outing, usually a meal. It is a major 'get together' funded by an employer to promote harmony and goodwill among employees.

Origin: These days such outings are better known as 'bonding' or 'team-building' exercises. An annual outing would be arranged on special occasions such as an anniversary or at the end of the financial year. 'Bean' feast relates to the bean goose. These birds usually arrive in Britain in large numbers during the autumn and, centuries ago, they were served at Christmas before turkeys became the festive dish of choice. They were known as the 'bean goose' because of the bean-shaped markings on its bill.

A blue ribbon event

Meaning: Highest distinction or prominence.

Origin: In Britain the highest award for merit is a knighthood. Foremost among the orders of knighthood is the Most Noble Order of the Garter, so called because of the garter of dark blue velvet ribbon worn by recipients.

A blue stocking

Meaning: The expression is used to describe a clever and intellectual woman.

Origin: In Venice in 1400, a secret society of high-minded men and women was formed calling themselves *della calza*, which means 'of the stocking'. They created a crest, which had blue stockings as its emblem. This proved to be very popular with the ladies of intellect.

A bunch of fives

Meaning: A fist. The fives are the five fingers.

Origin: The phrase appears in print in 1825, in Charles Westmacott's *The English Spy*: 'With their bunch of fives.'

A bistro

Meaning: A fast-food café.

Origin: After the defeat of Napoleon at the Battle of Waterloo troops from all over Europe began to occupy Paris, particularly the Russians. Naturally the French cafés were soon bustling with new visitors, trade was roaring and one of the most frequent shouts to be heard at the time was *'bweestra, bweestra'* which means 'quickly' in Russian. Hence the word soon became associated with cheap bars, small clubs and cafés.

A bunny boiler

Meaning: A former lover, always female, who refuses to accept a relationship is over and will go to any lengths to make her man pay dearly for the rejection. She is an unhinged and dangerous woman.

Origin: The expression originates from the film *Fatal Attraction* (1987), starring Michael Douglas and Glenn Close.

A chip off the old block

Meaning: A child who is just like his father or mother, in both appearance and character.

Origin: The obvious reference is to a chip of wood taken from a larger block, suggesting the carpenter cut off a small piece of wood that was exactly the same in every way to the larger piece, except in size.

A Collins

Meaning: A letter of thanks to a person for his/her hospitality.

Origin: The word was widely used in the 1800s after the novelist Jane Austen had one of her characters, in *Pride and Prejudice* (1813), threatening to send such a letter to the Bennet family following a stay at their country house. The character in question was a sycophantic clergyman called Mr Collins. These days it also called a 'Bread and Butter Letter'.

A damp squib

Meaning: Something of an anticlimax.

Origin: A 'squib' is a small firework thrown by hand, and a damp one is hardly likely to excite anybody awaiting the loud pops and bangs of proper fireworks. They are bound to be disappointed.

A diehard supporter

Meaning: Resilient, fierce and will show complete loyalty in any circumstances.

Origin: The original group of 'diehards' were the British 57th Foot Regiment, in the Duke of Wellington's army, who fought bravely against the French during the Battle of Albuhera. On 16 May 1811, their commanding officer, Colonel Inglis, had his horse shot dead from beneath him and he himself lay badly injured on the ridge that was a key position for Wellington's army. At that time, the English were outnumbered by French troops and under heavy attack. But even so, Inglis refused all attempts to carry him to the rear and instead lay shouting encouragement to his men: 'Die Hard the 57th, Die Hard.'

A dog day

Meaning: A very hot day that makes us lazy.

Origin: The Romans called it *Canicularis Dies*, the days between 3 July and 11 August, when the dog star Sirius rises at the same time as the sun. According to the Romans, these were the hottest days of the year.

A dog in a manger

Meaning: Someone who is not prepared to allow others to benefit from something that they themselves cannot use.

Origin: In one of *Aesop's Fables* we find a tale about an ox and a dog that were stabled together for the night. Both were starving hungry and the only food available was the hay in the manger. Dogs do not eat hay but the ox happily does! Thus the jealous hound began snapping and biting at him. The dog sat in the manger and would not allow the ox to eat, preferring instead to deprive his friend of the hay.

A dog in the night-time

Meaning: An unsuspecting conniver, someone who has unwittingly involved themselves in a crime.

Origin: Sir Arthur Conan Doyle invented the dog in question when he published the Sherlock Holmes adventure 'Silver Blaze' in 1892. In the story, the family dog would not bark during the night when horses were being stolen from the stable because it knew the man who had taken them.

A dish fit for gods

Meaning: An offering of high quality.

Origin: From Shakespeare's *Julius Caesar*, 1601. In his famous speech Brutus expresses the view that, although the conspirators are resolved to kill Caesar, they aren't mere butchers and should leave his body in a suitable state for the gods to view.

A draconian measure

Meaning: A harsh and old-fashioned punishment, law or rule.

Origin: The expression actually derives from the Draconian Code, which could be found in Athens in the seventh century BC at a time when the authorities appointed Draco to oversee law and order and apply punishment in the name of the state. Draco drew up a code of laws that were so severe that almost any crime was considered to be a capital offence, punishable by death.

A drop in the bucket

Meaning: A very small proportion of the whole.

Origin: 'A drop in the bucket' is the predecessor of 'a drop in the ocean', which means the same thing.

A feather in one's cap

Meaning: A symbol of honour and achievement.

Origin: The placing of a feather in a hat has been a symbol of achievement that has arisen in several cultures. The Native American tradition of adding a feather to the head-dress of any warrior who performed a brave act is well known.

A fish rots from the head down

Meaning: When an organization or state fails, it is the leadership that is the root cause.

Origin: It was first in a Greek text by Erasmus, who died in 1546. All of the early examples of the phrase in print in English prefer the 'a fish stinks from the head down'. The Turks have a homely proverb applied on such occasions; they say 'the fish stinks first at the head', meaning, that if the servant is disorderly, it is because the master is so.

A foot in the door

Meaning: An introduction or way in to something, made in order that progress may be made later.

Origin: 'Foot in the door' in a figurative sense, with a similar meaning to 'the thin end of the wedge', was the technique of jamming a foot in the door to prevent it closing, used by door-to-door salesmen and political canvassers.

A golden key can open the door

Meaning: Money opens any door.

Origin: This notion must be as old as money itself.

A hatchet job

Meaning: A brutal and unpleasant task carried out by Hatchet Men.

Origin: The origins can be found in the American gang warfare of the 1920s. When the Chinese drug gangs began arriving in US cities, Chinese gang leaders and outwardly respectable businessmen would sometimes hire a man with a hatchet to murder rivals. The expression 'hatchet men' was later applied to hired gunmen and extended into commerce, followed inevitably by politics and journalism, where it is still used as a term to describe anybody hired to destroy someone's reputation or credibility.

A hooray Henry

Meaning: A loud mouthed, upper-class, public school idiot.

Origin: Jim Godbolt coined the phrase in 1951 when he used it to describe the fans of Old Etonian jazz trumpeter Humphrey Lyttelton who would turn up in droves to the 100 Club in Oxford Street, London, to hear him play. Between songs, Lyttelton's supporters could be identified by the loud, upper-class voices shouting, 'Hooray, Hooray.'

A legend in one's own time

Meaning: Literal meaning, that is, a living person of considerable fame.

Origin: The original use of this phrase was 'a legend in her life time', written of Florence Nightingale by Lytton Strachey, in his well-known book *Eminent Victorians*, 1918. The 'own' is now almost always added to make 'a legend in his/her own lifetime.'

A little bird told me

Meaning: A phrase we use when we do not want to reveal the source of our information but most people could be expected to guess correctly anyway.

Origin: Used since the mid-16th century and is thought to have its root in a charming little story from the Book of Kings in the Bible about a meeting between the Queen of Sheba and King Solomon. Once upon a time all the birds in the land were summoned to appear before the great King Solomon, which they duly did. Well, all apart from a small lapwing whose absence could not be explained by any of the other birds. When the lapwing finally appeared, she was questioned about her absence and explained she had been to visit the Queen of Sheba and that the queen was making preparations to visit King Solomon. The king was pleased with the news and began to make preparations at court to receive his guest. Meanwhile, the little bird flew off to Ethiopia and told the queen that the king had a great desire to meet her and so she excitedly began making plans for the trip. The famed meeting thus took place thanks to the lap wing. When King Solomon asked the Queen of Sheba how the visit had been arranged, she replied, 'A little bird told me.' The King, of course, had to admit that 'a little bird' had told him too.

A loose cannon

Meaning: Unreliable, unpredictable and dangerous.

Origin: This is American in origin and related to US artillerymen that fired their cannons during the Civil War both randomly and inaccurately, sometimes even at their own men.

A lush

Meaning: Persons who drink a little more than is good for them.

Origin: In the mid-18th century 'lush' was a slang word for beer.

A lynch mob

Meaning: A group of people determined to take the law into their own hands and dispense summary justice, initially in the form of beatings and then executions by hanging.

Origin: A lynching and to lynch a person are connected terms, but in fact arose after the expression 'lynch mob'. These mobs (vigilante groups of men) in the southern states of America were as much a part of life in the late 19th century as the cowboys were. In ten states alone, authorities recorded 2,805 deaths at the hands of the mobs between 1882 and 1930. Of the victims, 2,500 were blacks, hanged without trial by white lynch mobs.

A man of straw

Meaning: A frontman of an enterprise who appears to be in a position of authority but in reality is controlled by others who are less visible.

Origin: In modern times they are more likely to be thought of as puppets or figureheads. The expression can be traced to the law courts and the dubious practice of men and women who would attend court each day in the hope they would be employed by lawyers and swear on oath anything that was asked of them, in return for a fee. They would sit around waiting for lawyers to call for them and could be identified by the straw they stuffed into their shoes.

A maverick

Meaning: This refers to an unorthodox individual who is independent-minded and quite innovative.

Origin: Samuel Augustus Maverick (July 23, 1803—September 2, 1870) was a Texas lawyer, politician, land baron and signer of the Texas Declaration of Independence. His name is the source of the term maverick, first cited in 1867, which means independent-minded.

A navvy

Meaning: A manual worker or labourer who is employed on a casual basis for a fixed span of time.

Origin: During the Industrial Revolution, teams of manual labourers were employed throughout England to build the canal waterways, followed by the railway system. The canals were known as 'navigation networks' at the time and all the men employed to dig them termed 'navigators'. The word was soon abbreviated to 'navvy' and applied to anybody providing labour on the networks, whether water or rail.

All agog

Meaning: Excited, in high spirits.

Origin: From the French 'en gogues', meaning 'in mirth'.

All at sea

Meaning: In a state of confusion and disorder.

Origin: This is an extension of the nautical phrase 'at sea'. Any ship that was out of sight of land was in an uncertain position and in danger of becoming lost.

All grist to the mill

Meaning: Anything that might be able to turn us a profit. All little extra profits in any industry are known as 'grist to the mill'.

Origin: 'Grist' is the name given by the millers to the actual quantity of grain that can be put through the mill at any one time. In this literal sense, 'all grist to the mill' means everything will be ground, sawdust and all, with no leftovers and therefore maximum profit.

A red rag to a bull

Meaning: A deliberate provocation, sure to bring about an adverse reaction.

Origin: In the 17th century, to wave a red rag at someone was merely to chatter with them — 'red rag' was then a slang term for the tongue.

A skeleton in the cupboard

Meaning: A secret source of shame which if exposed can be hazardous for the reputation of a family and so a person or family makes efforts to conceal.

Origin: The phrase 'a skeleton in the closet' was coined in England in the 19th century. Since then the word 'closet' has been used primarily in England to mean 'water closet', that is, lavatory — a possible hiding place for a skeleton. The English now usually use 'a skeleton in the cupboard', with 'skeleton in the closet' more common in the USA.

A shot in the arm

Meaning: A stimulus.

Origin: This expression derives from the invigorating effect of injecting drugs. A shot is of course US slang for an injection, either of a narcotic or medicinal drug.

A stone's throw

Meaning: A short distance.

Origin: A stone's throw is, of course, literally the distance that a stone can be thrown, but has come to mean any short but undefined distance.

A woman needs a man like a fish needs a bicycle

Meaning: A feminist slogan, suggesting that men are superfluous to women's needs.

Origin: This slogan is often attributed to Gloria Steinem.

A word is your shell-like

Meaning: I would like to talk to you.

Origin: 'Shell-like' has been used to mean a person's ear since the late 19th century. Clearly this just refers to the ear's shape.

Apple-pie order

Meaning: Tidy and well-ordered.

Origin: The phrase may originate from the French *'nappes pliees'* i.e. neatly folded, or from 'cap-a-pie order'.

Away with the fairies

Meaning: Not facing reality; in a dream world.

Origin: This phrase has its basis in the Scots/Irish Gaelic tradition of belief in a set of folk myths, the cartoon version of which is a belief in the existence of 'the little people'.

Armed to the teeth

Meaning: Fully prepared for a confrontation.

Origin: Medieval warriors were often so laden with weapons that sometimes they would have to carry one in their teeth.

An ace in a hole

Meaning: A hidden advantage or a secret source of influence.

Origin: It is an American phrase that was used as the title of a Cole Porter song in one of his shows, *Let's Face It*, in 1941. It began with the popular card game, stud poker. The rules state that after each round of betting, every player (of which there can be up to ten) is dealt one more card face upwards with the exception of the last player, who is dealt a card face downwards, known as the 'hole card'. The winner of the game is determined by whoever has either the highest or the lowest-scoring hand, and the two share the pot (the winnings). An ace in the 'hole' (or up your sleeve) is obviously a huge and hidden advantage to a gambler.

An apple a day keeps the doctor away

Meaning: Literally keep fit by eating an apple everyday.

Origin: This was a catchy rhyme; a proverb from Pembrokeshire, or Devon. The earliest recording of the phrase, in 1866, states, 'Eat an apple on going to bed, And you'll keep the doctor from earning his bread'. But in 1913, Elizabeth Wright recorded this phrase from the latter: 'Ait a happle avore gwain to bed, An' you'll make the doctor beg his bread' or as the more popular version runs: 'An apple a day, keeps the doctor away.'

At one fell sweep

Meaning: All at once.

Origin: A 'swoop' is the sudden descent of a bird of prey on its victim. 'Fell' is from the Old French word *fell*, meaning 'merciless'.

A right-hand man

Meaning: An influential person's second in command, someone who is both indispensable and heavily relied upon.

Origin: Traditionally, a senior servant or assistant would be given the privilege of sitting or standing on the right-hand side of his master. This was not only a show of faith and trust, as from that position the servant could disable his master's sword arm (usually his right) and overcome him with ease, but also because the servant was in the best place to defend his master.

An Englishman's home is his castle

Meaning: A person's home is private, sacrosanct and to be protected at all costs.

Origin: In the Middle Ages, there was an old law that prevented any person from forcing entry to a private dwelling to carry out an arrest or to seize goods and chattels. That same law prevented the bailiffs of the High Sheriff from breaking in and helping themselves to a person's goods, and it is still the case that no bailiff is allowed to enter a private dwelling without first obtaining a court order.

A sop to Cerberus

Meaning: When someone bribes another to cool him/her down.

Origin: As the legend goes Cerberus was a three-headed dog and was a monster in Greek mythology. He guarded the gates of the underworld so only dead people could get in. However, he didn't let people go because he wanted to be bribed. A sop is a cake, or a honey cake. Cerberus was given this to come down to the underworld. While he ate the sop one could slip in! The Romans were kept in a crypt with a piece of cake in their hand.

As the crow flies

Meaning: The shortest distance between two points.

Origin: A crow, the navy believed, would always fly straight for the nearest point of land, once it had been released from the top of a mast. That is why there is a 'crow's nest' up there.

A storm in a tea cup

Meaning: A petty argument or fight over nothing serious that is quickly resolved.

Origin: The Roman orator and statesman Cicero wrote '*excitabat fluctus in simpulo*', which, translated literally, means 'he whipped up waves in a ladle'.

A slush fund

Meaning: Money collected with little effort, or money from an investment or funding scheme that has been designated for any other.

Origin: The original slush fund was found in galley kitchens beneath decks on the tall ships of the 17th and 18th centuries. In those pre-refrigerated days, meat would be preserved for many months by being salted and stored in wooden barrels.

A silly billy

Meaning: A phrase used affectionately to describe a person, usually a child, who is up to some kind of mischief.

Origin: The original Billy was King George III's uncle William Frederick, the Duke of Gloucester (1776—1834), who was known to be of weak intellect and managed to get up to all sorts of embarrassing and stupid antics at court. The word 'silly' derives from the Old English word *soelig*, meaning 'happy' or 'blessed' and during the Middle-Ages; it was pronounced 'seely' in many English dialects. By then, the word had changed to mean feeble, unsophisticated and ignorant.

Ashes to ashes and dust to dust

Meaning: This expression is used at every funeral service.

Origin: The ashes do not refer to the remains of a cremation, however, and the dust is nothing to do with a burial. Instead they relate to the practice, dating back to Biblical times, of those in mourning, who sprinkled earth or sand (dust) and ashes over their heads at the funeral of a loved one.

A stool pigeon

Meaning: An informer or a police spy.

Origin: This is a hunting expression and reveals the common practice of tying (sometimes even nailing) a pigeon to a high stool as a decoy for other pigeons, which would then land nearby and be at the mercy of waiting hunters. The expression was in regular use by 1825.

A tea caddy

Meaning: A place where we store our tea leaves or tea bags.

Origin: The phrase derives from the Malaysian word *kati* for the measurement, slightly over a pound, of tea traditionally sold throughout Southeast Asia. A 'tea-*kati*' would be what was brought home from the market. The popular idiom used for an errand boy, or something that 'carries'; this could also have something to do with the expression 'caddy' in golf.

A ten gallon hat

Meaning: A hat that the cowboy American ranch workers and cowboys would wear to shield them from the heat of the sun as they went about their work on the plains.

Origin: It was John B. Stetson (1830—1906) who popularized the broad-brimmed hat when his company, founded in Philadelphia in 1865, began producing the Stetson or, as it was sometimes called, the John B. The nickname 'ten gallon hat' was introduced in the late 1800s as a reflection on its capacity to carry large quantities of water, although this is a slight exaggeration.

A tomboy

Meaning: A young girl who behaves more as a boy might do.

Origin: Used in the 16th century. The word derives from the old Anglo-Saxon word *tumbere*, which means 'dancer' or 'romper' and is from the same root at the French word *tomber*, which means 'to fall' or 'tumble', which also gave us 'tom rig', a 17th century term for a prostitute or 'loose woman'.

A turncoat

Meaning: One who will change his loyalty and soon switch sides without a moment's hesitation.

Origin: The term turncoat refers to retreating soldiers who turned their coats around and wore them back to front in the hope nobody would realize they were actually running away rather than still facing the enemy.

At logger heads

Meaning: In dispute with.

Origin: A 'logger-head' was literally a 'block-head'. A logger was a thick block of timber which was fastened to a horse's leg to prevent it from running away.

At sixes and sevens

Meaning: To be in a state of disorder, unable to complete a task effectively.

Origin: In 1327 two of the great livery companies, the Skinners and the Merchant Taylors, each received their charter within a few days of the other. But an argument immediately broke out as to which of the two firms was to be placed at number six in the order of companies going on processions in the City of London, and which would be the seventh. The matter was resolved when it was suggested each company should share the coveted number six position by swapping places every year. This went on until 1484 when the masters of both firms submitted the matter to the then Mayor of London for his judgment. Rather than getting bogged down in all the rights and wrongs of the affair, the Mayor decided a simple solution would be for the masters and wardens of both companies to entertain each other to dinner once a year, as well as continuing to alternate their places on the processions.

Anybody who is gung ho

Meaning: One who is bullish and aggressive and highly enthusiastic.

Origin: This originally applied to Carlson's Raiders, who were a moderately successful marine guerrilla unit operating in the South Pacific during the Second World War between 1942 and 1946. Their commanding officer, Evans F. Carlson, spent many years in China prior to the war, developing his battle strategies by observing Chinese teamwork and comradeship. In China the term *kung ho* means 'working closely together' and this is where Carlson found his phrase.

AWOL

Meaning: A friend or colleague whose absence cannot be explained. Literally it stands for 'absent without leave'.

Origin: Originally, in military terms the expression meant 'missing without permission'; it was applied to soldiers who were absent for a short period of time and then returned to their ranks. During the American Civil War, offenders were forced to wear a placard around their necks with the initials AWOL printed on it, which stood for 'Absent without Leave'. As they were not strictly deserters, the only punishment they had to endure was public shame.

A wolf in sheep's clothing

Meaning: Someone who is not quite what they appear to be at first glance.

Origin: This expression, which has been much used over the centuries, can be found in one of *Aesop's Fables*, dating back 1,400 years. The story tells of a wolf that wraps himself up in a sheep's fleece and sneaks past the shepherd, into the paddock, disguised as one of the flock. Once inside, he immediately eats up one of the lambs before his deception can be revealed. But the origin of the expression can be found in the Bible (*Matthew 7:15*), which states: 'Beware of false prophets, which come to you in sheep's clothing. Inwardly they are ravening wolves.'

B

Back seat drivers

Meaning: Someone who criticizes from the sidelines.

Origin: This comes from the annoying habit of some people giving unwanted advice to vehicle drivers.

Back to square one

Meaning: Back to the beginning, to start again.

Origin: This goes back to board games like Snakes and Ladders and playground games like hopscotch.

Back to the drawing board

Meaning: Start again on a new design or plan after the failure of an earlier attempt.

Origin: This term has been used since WWII—a design has failed and that a new one is needed. A drawing board is, of course, an architect's or draughtsman's table, used for the preparation of designs or blueprints.

Bad books

Meaning: Out of favour.

Origin: In the Middle Ages, 'one's books' meant 'one's reckoning or cognizance'. So to be 'out of someone's books' meant you were no longer part of their life or of interest to them.

A bad egg

Meaning: Someone or something that disappoints expectations.

Origin: The allusion is clearly to the disappointment felt when cracking or shelling an egg, only to find that it is bad.

Bag and baggage

Meaning: All of one's possessions.

Origin: The phrase is of military origin. 'Bag and baggage' refers to the entire property of an army and that of the soldiers too. To 'retire bag and baggage' meant to beat an honourable retreat, surrendering nothing.

Baker's dozen

Meaning: Thirteen.

Origin: It's widely believed that this phrase originated from the practice of medieval English bakers giving an extra loaf when selling a dozen in order to avoid being penalized for selling short weight.

Balance of powers

Meaning: The distribution of power between nations in such a way that no single state has dominance over the others.

Origin: Of uncertain origin, but dating back to at least the early 18th century; for example, this piece from the *The London Gazette*, 1701: 'Your Glorious Design of Re-establishing a just Balance of Power in Europe.'

Bald as a badger

Meaning: Absolutely bald.

Origin: These are phrases used regularly in both America and Britain respectively, the latter having been in use since around 1430. The aquatic coot is often known as the 'bald coot' because of the white flash on the bird's head that is thought to resemble a man's bald pate. The badger simile, on the other hand, has been shortened over time and in fact started life as 'bald as a badger's bum'. The reason for this is that for centuries the bristles on a gentleman's shaving brush were made out of luxurious badger's hair, plucked from the poor creature's backside.

Ball and chain

Meaning: A heavy metal ball to tie a prisoner to prevent his escape.

Origin: This rather crude description of a wife refers to the ball and chain strapped to a prisoner's leg in American and British prisons in the early 19th century.

Balls to the wall

Meaning: Pushed to the limit.

Origin: It derives from aviation. The 'balls' sat on top of the levers controlling the throttle and fuel mixtures; pushing them forward toward the front wall of the cockpit made the plane go faster.

Bandy around

Meaning: To argue, discuss in a lively fashion.

Origin: Bandy was a medieval bat-and-ball game, similar to hockey. To 'bandy' words is to knock them back and forth as one would bandy a ball.

Bank holidays

Meaning: Most employees, apart from those in the service sector, are given the day off.

Origin: Today these are officially known as 'public holidays', but the original expression is still in general use across the world. It all started at the Bank of England in the 19th century. Until 1830, the world's premier bank was closed for more than 40 days in every 12 months. But during that year the number was dropped to 18 and only four years later reduced again to just four. Now they appear to have settled upon eight. They are: New Year's Day, Good Friday, Easter Monday, May Day, the spring and August hank holidays, Christmas Day and Boxing Day.

Baptism of fire

Meaning: A severe introduction to a new situation.

Origin: The actual phrase can be traced back as far as the mid-16th century and the purge by the Catholics of the heretic Christians who were martyred over the following century for their beliefs, by being burned at the stake. The Catholics had believed the Christians would learn of their lifetime 'crimes against God' at the gates of heaven and then be converted to Catholicism. Hence the sneering phrase, 'this is your baptism, a baptism of fire'.

Barbecue

Meaning: A wooden framework for storing meat on or laying fish out to be dried.

Origin: It derives from the Spanish word *barbacoa*, or possibly from the same word in the West Indian Arawak language, both meaning 'wooden frame on posts'. On this framework a large animal would be turned from time to time and roasted over an open fire.

Barking mad

Meaning: Insanity, craziness or madness is a spectrum of behaviours characterized by certain abnormal mental or behavioural patterns. Insanity may manifest as violations of societal norms, including a person becoming a danger to themselves or others, though not all such acts are considered insanity.

Origin: This phrase is a reference to rabid dogs, barking in their madness. A more interesting (but less likely) tale is that 'barking mad' originates from the east London suburb of Barking, where there was an asylum for the insane during the medieval period.

Bare-faced lie

Meaning: A lie told without any shame or guilt.

Origin: In its original form, this expression indicated a fresh honesty, as a clean-shaven face could not conceal any untruths or hidden meanings, whereas all manner of slyness and duplicity could be hidden beneath a beard. In time, the phrase came to describe a person who didn't care whether or not they were lying and had no real intention of concealing their deception.

Barking up the wrong tree

Meaning: Making a mistake or a false assumption in something you are trying to achieve.

Origin: The allusion is to hunting dogs barking at the bottom of trees where they mistakenly think their quarry is hiding.

Basket case

Meaning: In a completely hopeless or useless condition.

Origin: In World War I the expression was used to describe servicemen who had all of their limbs surgically removed or whose limbs had been lost in an explosion—leaving them with only torsos. They would then have to be carried in a basket.

Bats in the belfry

Meaning: An English way of describing the harmlessly insane, eccentric or mentally challenged.

Origin: The allusion is to bats flapping around in the bell tower of a church or cathedral in a wild and frenzied manner once the ringing has woken them up.

Beam's end

Meaning: Hard up; in a bad situation.

Origin: The beams here are the horizontal transverse timbers of ships. This nautical phrase came about with the allusion to the danger of imminent capsize if the beam ends were touching the water.

Bear up

Meaning: To keep your spirits high and remain cheerful when things aren't going well or determined to show of self-confidence in the face of adversity.

Origin: In nautical language the term 'bear up' means to steer a sailing ship more closely into the wind, which is more challenging than steering away from the wind (or 'bearing off'). This also derives probably from the carriage horses that were used in the days before motorized transport. The 'bearing rein' was part of the harness used to hold a horse's neck in a proud, upright position during ceremonies. When, at the end of a long exhausting parade, a horse began to show signs of fatigue, the bearing rein was used to pull its head back into position and the poor animal was known to be bearing upwards.

Beat around the bush

Meaning: To avoid answering a question or to approach something in a roundabout way.

Origin: In the 1500s hunters hired people called 'beaters' to drive small animals such as birds, rabbits and foxes out of bushes so the hunters could get a better shot at them, being careful not to drive the animals out into the open before the hunters arrived. They used their long sticks, hitting around the bushes rather than directly on them.

Bedlam

Meaning: A place of uncontrollable confusion and uproar.

Origin: In 1247, the Priory of St Mary of Bethlehem was established in London and 300 years later, in 1547, the building was given to the city by Henry VIII as a hospital called Bethlem, used to house the mentally unstable and insane. The asylum became known as 'Bedlam'.

Beefeaters

Meaning: Servants.

Origin: The Tower of London is traditionally guarded by Yeoman Warders, who have been called Beefeaters since the latter half of the 15th century. Henry VIII appointed them as warders at the Tower of London, called the Yeomen Extraordinary of the Guard, during the early 16th century. Around that time servants were called 'beefeaters' with those of a slightly higher rank labeled 'loaf eaters'. In keeping with their elevated status, the Yeoman Warders became known at the Tower as 'Beefeaters' reflecting the generous meat rations they were given.

Bee's knees

Meaning: To be regarded as the best, superior to everyone (or everything) else.

Origin: Once a bee has flown into a flower, pollen sticks to its body and the insect then carefully transfers it to sacs on its rear legs. The term stems from the delicate way in which bees bend those diminutive leg joints to perform this task. Note: 'as busy as a bee', meaning to work hard at something, 'making a beeline' meaning to go directly for something. The phrase derives from the ancient belief that a bee always flew in a straight line from its nectar gathering to the hive, although that piece of folklore has since been proved to be untrue. 'A bee in your bonnet' describes the manner of someone who is flapping around and making a fuss, as you might if there were actually a bee in your hat. 'The queen bee' is the lady who believes herself to be, or is believed to be, in charge of everyone else. The Greek philosopher Plato was known as the 'athenian bee', so called because of the legend that, as a baby, a swarm of bees settled on his mouth when he was still in his cradle, so that all his words flowed with the sweetness of honey. Meanwhile Sophocles, the Greek tragic poet, was known as the 'Attic bee' due to the sweetness of his sonnets and, as some believe, the place in his house where he wrote them, although 'Attic' in this instance means 'relating to ancient Athens' which is where both Sophocles and Plato hailed from.

Before you say jack knife

Meaning: In a very short time; suddenly.

Origin: Jack Robinson was a mythical figure and no more real than Jack Tar, Jack Frost or Jack the Giant Killer.

Benchmark

Meaning: A standard of quality and performance; to set an A level.

Origin: In the days of the great Greek and Roman builders and engineers, a 'benchmark' was a vital feature of any building project, the technology then being introduced to Britain. A benchmark was, and technically still is for that matter, a series of broad, arrow-shaped marks carved vertically into an existing stone building or large rock.

Before you can say Jack Robinson

Meaning: Before you can say Jack Robinson, it'll all be over.

Origin: In 1778, Fanny Burney first used the expression in her novel *Evelina*. In the text, Fanny indicates the phrase is already well-known in the way she regularly uses it to describe something that happens 'in an instant'.

Better late than never

Meaning: To arrive or do something later than expected isn't good, but it is better than not at all.

Origin: This proverb is often expressed with a degree of sarcasm, apparently saying something positive but in fact merely remarking on someone's lateness.

Between a rock and a hard place

Meaning: Out of options.

Origin: It's a somewhat inaccurate reference to the Greek epic poem, *The Odyssey*. There's a passage where the hero has to choose whether to sail close to the monster Scylla or the whirlpool Charybdis.

Big brother

Meaning: Being watched over by the authorities at all times.

Origin: In 1948, George Orwell wrote his classic novel *Nineteen Eighty-Four* in which the government exercises dictatorial control by watching every move of its citizens. Orwell called this cynical, oppressive head of a totalitarian state, Big Brother.

Birthday suit

Meaning: To be one of complete nakedness, suggesting this was the 'suit' we were born in.

Origin: The original 'birthday suit' or at least the one the expression referred to in the first place, is a specially commissioned suit of clothes worn by all royal courtiers on the reigning monarch's birthday. While that tradition has long since died out, the expression remains with us.

Bite the bullet

Meaning: Face up to unpleasant reality.

Origin: Before anesthetics were invented, injured soldiers would bite on a bullet to help them endure the pain of an operation/amputation.

Bitten the dust

Meaning: Something that is worn out, broken down or even dead.

Origin: The expression became widespread thanks to the American cowboy movies so popular in the early part of the 20th century. Although the phrase originally applied to warriors (or indeed cowboys) who died in battle; it is now frequently used to describe almost anything that is no longer any use to us.

Black dog moods

Meaning: Periods of depression and sullen spirits.

Origin: The expression was popularized during the 1930s and 1940s by Winston Churchill, who famously suffered from bouts of depression, which he called his 'black dogs'.

Black sheep

Meaning: Black sheep of the family is generally regarded as a disgrace different from the rest and with a rogue element implied.

Origin: Down the years, a black lamb in a flock was always the unpopular one as its fleece could not be dyed and was therefore less valuable than those of the white lambs.

Black Tuesday

Meaning: When panic sets in.

Origin: This a well-known expression used to describe 29 October 1929, which is the day panic set in at the New York Stock Exchange. That is how the adjective 'black' began to be broadly used to describe an unforgettably bad day such as 'Black Friday'.

Blackmail

Meaning: To blackmail somebody is to demand money by threats, usually to expose secrets.

Origin: It was the 1600s that this word originated from the Highlands of Scotland. The 'mail' in blackmail is the old Scottish word for 'rent', usually spelt either *maill* or *male*; in Old Norse the word *mal* meant 'agreement' or 'contract'. In those days, tenants paid their rent in silver coins. This used to be known as 'white money'. But in the 17th century Highland clans began a protection racket for farmers and traders. This informal tax, additional rent, soon came to be known as 'black money' or 'black rent', being the opposite of 'white rent'. Hence 'blackmail' became part of the English language as a word used to describe the practice of obtaining money by threat of violence. Those unable to pay would have their stock confiscated and this would then be sold on the black market.

Blowing hot and cold

Meaning: Undecided and inconsistent in their actions.

Origin: In Classical mythology it referred to a traveller who was given food and shelter by a kindly satyr (a woodland god with the horns, tail and legs of a goat and an attendant of Bacchus, the god of wine and lustfulness). According to the legend, the satyr gave the traveller a room for the night and some hot soup. The man blew on his fingers to warm them and then, with the same breath, blew on the soup to cool it. Irritated at the man's apparent indecision, the satyr packed him off outside and sent him back on his travels.

Blood is thicker than water

Meaning: Suggests that family bonds of trust and loyalty are stronger than those friendships we make for ourselves.

Origin: In ancient Middle Eastern culture, blood rituals symbolized bonds that were far greater than those of the family. Hence the bond between Blood Brothers—warriors who symbolically share the blood they have shed together in battle—is far stronger than the one between you and the boy you grew up with. In addition, there is an expression dating back three thousand years that tells us: 'The blood of the covenant is far stronger than the water of the womb', which is a forerunner of the phrase we use today. In modern times, we understand 'blood' to be the bloodline of a family.

Blot your copybook

Meaning: To make a mistake, but not a particularly serious one.

Origin: It means you are out of favour for a while until you can make amends. The expression originates from the time children used to learn to write using the newly introduced fountain pens and inkwells. Schools would provide children with two writing books, one for rough work, which could be full of crossed-out mistakes, misspellings and ink blots, and a copybook, which would be used for the finished work and presented to the teacher for appraisal. Children would be punished, although not severely, for 'blotting their copybooks' with ink stains.

Blow the gaff

Meaning: To reveal a secret of some sort or to inform on a person.

Origin: At carnivals and fairgrounds during the 18th century, operators would use a concealed device in games in order to reduce a customer's chance of winning. In carnival slang this was known as a gaff. It is also recorded that around that time the word 'blow' was slang for 'reveal' or 'expose' and therefore to expose the hidden deception at the carnival became known as 'blowing the gaff'.

Blown to smithereens

Meaning: Shattered into thousands of small pieces.

Origin: This expression is of Gaelic origin, 'smithereens' meaning 'small or tiny fragments'. The Gaelic spelling of the word, *smidirin*, leads us to a modern Irish expression for severe hangovers.

Blue blooded

Meaning: Term is used to describe people who are from royal or aristocratic families; those who consider themselves socially superior.

Origin: In 711, the Moors invaded Spain for the first time and for many centuries much of the country was under Moorish rule. During the Middle Ages, fair-skinned Europeans called all Asian people, and indeed darker-skinned Mediterranean folk, 'Moors', and in Spain, members of the aristocracy, with particularly pale skin as the result of never intermarrying with 'Moors', were termed *Sangre Azul*, which may be translated literally as Blue Blood. This is because the veins under the skin appear much bluer in paler-skinned people, leading to the belief that the white Spanish nobility must be fundamentally different from the Moors—whom the aristocracy considered to be socially inferior to themselves—and hence that their blood must also be blue in colour.

Blue chip company

Meaning: The most sought after and reliable.

Origin: In gaming houses and casinos across the world, players never use cash to gamble with. Instead, they lodge their money with a cashier in exchange for chips, so called because they were originally chips of wood, coloured in accordance with their value. The blue-coloured chips were initially the highest in value and consequently the most popular and secure.

Bob's your uncle

Meaning: Something that is resolved in your favor without much effort, as in: 'Just send the form in and Bob's your uncle.'

Origin: The phrase was in regular use in England from the 1890s after the promotion in 1886 of Arthur Balfour to Secretary of State for Ireland. Balfour was a surprise choice for the position and few regarded him as qualified for the post. But when it became known he was the nephew of British Prime Minister Robert Gascoyne-Cecil, 3rd Marquis of Salisbury, the joke circulated that if Robert was your uncle, then anything was possible.

Bolt from the blue

Meaning: A complete and unexpected surprise. Can you expect a thunderbolt in a blue sky?

Origin: The Romans termed a flash of lightning on a sunny day as a 'thunderbolt from the blue' and they would use this phrase figuratively to explain any kind of sudden surprise.

Bone up

Meaning: To study intensively and gain as much information about a matter, as possible.

Origin: The expression in fact derives from the translator and bibliographer Henry Bohn (1796–1884), who made his name as a secondhand bookseller and publisher of cheap editions and whose libraries served both students and the wider public. When his translations of the Classics were published, they became literary handbooks for students who were studying or 'cramming' ('Bohning up') for an examination.

Booby prize

Meaning: This is the prize given to a person or team who comes last in an event.

Origin: A 'booby' is in fact a slow-witted South American bird that is easy to catch. In the 17th century, sailors found that a simple noose set on deck with a few dried biscuits as bait was enough to trap the daft bird—hence the phrase booby trap. As an extension of this, slow-witted sailors were known as 'boobies' and consequently the prize for being in last place in a contest had to be a 'booby prize'.

Born with a silver spoon in your mouth

Meaning: To be born into a wealthy family.

Origin: It was traditional for godparents to present a newborn baby with the gift of a silver spoon, thereby providing the child's first 'taste' of wealth and good fortune. It could be said, however, that those born into a rich family had no need to wait for a godparent to make such a gift as they already had great wealth. They had been born with their own 'silver spoon,' as it were.

Boss

Meaning: A person in charge.

Origin: It derives from the Dutch word *baas*, translated as 'master', and is used to describe any person in charge, hence the expression 'to boss somebody around'.

Boxing day

Meaning: The day after Christmas, i.e. 26th December.

Origin: The day following Christmas Day was formerly known as St Stephen's Day. For centuries it was customary for religious folk to leave a box in church, during the Christmas Mass, which was packed full of gifts and money. The contents, known as 'the dole of the Christmas box' or 'the box money', would then be distributed by priests to the needy on the following day (St Stephen's Day), which subsequently became known as 'the box day'.

Brass monkey weather

Meaning: Very cold weather conditions.

Origin: Some references say that the brass triangles that supported stacks of iron cannonballs on sailing ships were called monkeys and that in cold weather the metal contracted, causing the balls to fall off.

Break the ice

Meaning: To initiate a project or even friendship.

Origin: In early days port cities that thrived on trade suffered during the winter because frozen rivers prevented commercial ships from entering the city. Small ships known as 'icebreakers' would rescue the icebound ships by breaking the ice and creating a path for them to follow. It has now become customary to 'break the ice' before beginning a project in any kind of business arrangement.

Bread is the staff of life

Meaning: Importance of bread as a staple of our daily diet.

Origin: Bread has featured symbolically in all religions and is frequently mentioned throughout the Bible, such as in *John 6:35*: 'And Jesus said unto them, I am the bread of life: he that cometh to me shall never hunger.'

Breaking bread together

Meaning: Sharing a meal and holding conversation in a open and friendly manner.

Origin: This expression can be traced to the Last Supper when Jesus sat down with his disciples, broke a loaf of bread and shared it around with some wine.

Break a leg

Meaning: Don't want to tempt fate by talking about positive outcomes in advance.

Origin: It is said that stage actors are very superstitious. They don't say 'Macbeth' in a theater, they don't whistle backstage, and they never wish each other 'good luck' before a performance. They tell each other to break a leg because they don't want to tempt fate by talking about positive outcomes in advance. Break a leg was heard in theater circles starting in the 1920s, and first appeared in print around 1954 or 1957. The idea behind the phrase is quite old, possibly dating from medieval belief in malevolent spirits, but break a leg itself is fairly recent. The phrase is similar to a German saying *hals und beinbruch*, meaning 'neck and leg break.' It's used to mean good luck. One theory is that German-speaking or Yiddish-speaking Jews brought the saying with them to America early in the 20th century. Many of these immigrants worked in theater, so the translated phrase spread.

Bring home the bacon

Meaning: Make a point with clarity.

Origin: This phrase is often attributed to the story of Dunmow Flitch. In 1104, a couple in Great Dunmow, Essex, impressed the Prior of Little Dunmow with their love and devotion so much, that he awarded them a flitch (a side of bacon).

Bronx cheer

Meaning: A sound of contempt or derision, made by blowing through closed lips, usually with the tongue protruding.

Origin: The Bronx is a borough of New York City, named after the 17th century Jonas Bronck, who was the first recorded European settler in the area. 'Bronx cheer' originated as a slang term in the USA in the early years of the 20th century and began appearing in newspapers from around 1920.

In the buff

Meaning: Naked.

Origin: A buff-coat was a light browny/yellow leather tunic worn by English soldiers up until the 17th century. The original meaning of 'in the buff' was simply to be wearing such a coat. Later on, 'in the buff' was used to mean naked, due to the colour of the skin, which is similar to the buff coat.

Burning the candle at both ends

Meaning: People exhausting themselves by getting up early for work and then working hard, late into the night.

Origin: In bygone days, before electricity could keep us illuminated all night long, clerks and tradesmen working after dark would often secure their candles in the middle (horizontally) and then light them at both ends. This would give them enough light to work by, but not for very long, so they would have to work harder and faster in these conditions. This gave rise to the expression that we still use today.

Bury your head in the sand

Meaning: Refuse to confront or acknowledge a problem.

Origin: This comes from the supposed habit of ostriches burying their heads in the sand when faced with attack by predators.

Bust your chops

Meaning: To give someone a hard time.

Origin: At one time it was considered cool to sport a long, ridiculous pair of mutton chop side burns. From America to England, to Russia and to even farther away than Russia. When some civilized global population had had enough of these peninsula-shaped patches of hair they punched them in the face and their 'chops got busted'.

Butter someone up

Meaning: To flatter someone.

Origin: An ancient Indian custom in which balls of clarified butter are thrown at idols of the gods to seek their favour.

By hook or by crook

Meaning: Achieving something by any means possible, whether honest or not.

Origin: 'Hook' in question is a blunt bill-hook and the 'crook' the hooked staff a shepherd used to gather his flock. In feudal England during the Middle Ages, a law was passed preventing the cutting down of trees or lopping of branches to make firewood. But the law permitted the poor to gather dead wood from forests and deemed anything they could collect with a blunt hook or shepherd's crook was allowable.

By and large

Meaning: On the whole; generally speaking; all things considered.

Origin: This originated in the days of sail. When the wind is blowing from some compass point behind a ship's direction of travel then it is said to be 'large'. When the wind is in that favourable 'large' direction the largest square sails may be set and the ship is able to travel in whatever downwind direction the captain sees fit. Sailors would say that to be 'by the wind' is to face into the wind or within six compass points of it.

C

Calamity Jane

Meaning: This is an affectionate name for a young girl who gets herself into all sorts of trouble without really meaning to.

Origin: The original Calamity Jane was Martha Jane Canary (1852–1903) of Deadwood in South Dakota, USA. She notoriously behaved like a cowboy and was, unsurprisingly, unlucky in love. Or, at least, her husbands were unlucky in love as 11 out of 12 of them died in suspicious circumstances. Calamity Jane dressed, swore, rode, drank and fought like a man. She also famously threatened 'calamity' to any man who offended her in the smallest of ways.

Call a person's bluff

Meaning: To test claims and issue a challenge to reveal the truth.

Origin: Poker, from which the phrase derives, is essentially a game of deception where each player pretends to have the winning hand and the others have to consider the truth of that assertion against the value of the cards in their own hand. Once play begins, the chips (money tokens) are placed on the table and then the chips are down (things are getting serious). The expression 'poker-faced', meaning to reveal no outward emotion, comes from this part of the game. Some players, suspecting others have a superior hand by the way they are upping the stakes (putting more chips on the table) may pass their cards back to the dealer, face down, so the others won't know how they have been betting. If something is very likely to happen, and can be foreseen, it might be thought of as being on the cards. But this expression has nothing to do with poker; instead it relates to the practice of fortune telling and reading tarot cards.

Call a spade a spade

Meaning: To speak plainly — to describe something as it really is.

Origin: It might be thought that this derives from the derogatory use of the slang term 'spade', meaning Negro, an American term originating in the 20th century.

Can't hold a candle

Meaning: A poor or low performer.

Origin: Before electricity, workers needed a second set of hands to hold a candle for them. Holding a candle was clearly a less challenging job, so someone who isn't even qualified to provide light to a competent worker obviously wouldn't be able to perform the task himself.

Carbon copy

Meaning: An exact duplicate.

Origin: The term 'carbon copy' derives from carbon paper, which was, and occasionally still is, used to make copies of typewritten documents.

Catbird seat

Meaning: In a superior or advantageous position.

Origin: This is an American phrase—which is unsurprising as the grey catbird which is the probable source of the phrase is a North American species (there's also an Australian catbird). It's one of a group of birds called the mimic thrushes. They include mockingbirds and, as you might expect, they are adept mimics. The catbird is named for its ability to mimic the sound of a cat's miaow.

Cat got your tongue

Meaning: Something said when a person is at a loss for words.

Origin: It seems to originate from the practice of cutting out the tongues of liars and blasphemers and feeding them to cats.

A cat has nine lives

Meaning: This is a proverb.

Origin: This is a proverb dating back to around 1546. The belief is that cats are naturally able to land safely upon their feet from whatever height they are dropped and this gives them an obvious ability to get out of all sorts of trouble. In ancient Egypt, as in many parts of the world, cats had the reputation of being the perfect rat catchers and were an important means of ridding a city of the plague-spreading vermin. In Egypt, cats were also regarded as sacred, associated with the trinity of mother, father and son, and it was believed that if you multiplied the sacred number of three by three, you had calculated the number of lives the revered cat actually had.

Catch-22

Meaning: A situation where a person has no choice at all.

Origin: The phrase began to be used in America following the publication of Joseph Heller's book of the same name in September 1961. In the story, Heller's central character, a Second World War bomber pilot called Captain John Yossarian, believed he could be relieved from active duty by claiming insanity. Although it was noted that in attempting to avoid any further missions, Yossarian was in fact proving he had all his wits about him after all, as the following extract shows: 'There was only one catch and that was Catch-22 which specified that any concern for one's own safety, in the face of dangers that were real and immediate, was the process of a rational mind.'

Caught on the horns of a dilemma

Meaning: Facing a choice of two equally unfavourable situations.

Origin: The Greek word *lemma* may be loosely translated as 'expectation' or 'guess' and a 'dilemma' is a double *lemma*, or 'double problem'. Greek philosophers compared this to the two horns of a bull, which can both cause damage. If you choose to protect yourself from one horn, the other is still as much of a danger potentially.

Caught red-handed

Meaning: To be caught doing something wrong.

Origin: In the olden days when someone butchered an animal that didn't belong to him, he had to be caught with the animal's blood on his hands to be convicted as per the law of those days. Being caught only with freshly cut meat did not make the person guilty.

Chalk and talk

Meaning: The traditional teaching method where the teacher stood at the front to address the class while writing on the blackboard with a stick of chalk.

Origin: A modern-day spin-off of 'chalk and cheese' is 'chalk and talk'.

Chance your arm

Meaning: Take a risk.

Origin: The arm in question refers to a stripe of military rank worn on the upper sleeve. Take a risk and you might be demoted, thereby losing a stripe.

Charley horse

Meaning: Leg cramp or stiffness.

Origin: 'Charley horse' (sometimes misspelled 'Charlie horse') is an American phrase and originated in the sport of baseball.

Chew the cud

Meaning: To chat, in an aimless manner.

Origin: Alternative versions of this are 'chew the fat' and 'chew the rag', etc. Cud is the part digested food that ruminant animals, notably cows, bring back into their mouths from their first stomach, to chew at leisure. The image is of slow and aimless mastication and the allusive use of the phrase refers to that.

Chinese whisper

Meaning: Inaccurate gossip; a sequence of repetitions of a story, each one differing slightly from the original, so that the final telling bears only a scant resemblance to the original.

Origin: It derives from the party game in which one person whispers a message to the person next to them and the story is then passed progressively to several others, with inaccuracies accumulating as the game goes on. The point of the game is the amusement obtained from the last player's announcement of the story they heard, that typically being nothing like the original. In the USA it is usually called 'telephone' or 'gossip'.

Chop and change

Meaning: To change and change again.

Origin: Chop is a now an archaic word which has been used for centuries to mean 'change suddenly'.

Chow down

Meaning: Eating like a dog or dog food.

Origin: 'Chow down' was first used by the US military during WWII. 'Chow' is a Chinese breed of dog, that became a western slang term for food due to the Chinese's reputation for eating dog meat.

Cloud nine

Meaning: In a state of blissful happiness.

Origin: The expression originated as one of the classifications of cloud which were defined by the US Weather Bureau in the 1950s, in which 'cloud nine' denotes the fluffy cumulonimbus type that are considered so attractive. This phrase actually derives from Buddhism and cloud nine is one of the stages of the progress to enlightenment of a bodhisattva (one destined to become a Buddha).

Cock and bull story

Meaning: A fanciful and unbelievable tale.

Origin: The Cock and the Bull were two of the main coaching inns in a town and the banter and rivalry between groups of travellers is said to have resulted in exaggerated and fanciful stories, which became known as 'cock and bull stories'. The two hostelries did, and still do, exist.

Come up trumps

Meaning: Be triumphant, victorious.

Origin: 'Come up trumps' is a variant of 'turn up trumps', which has been used since the early 17th century. 'Trump' is a corruption of triumph, which was the name of a popular card game during this period.

Chip on your shoulder

Meaning: A person who is looking for an argument or holding a grudge and provokes a physical challenge.

Origin: We say he has a chip on his shoulder. Someone who remains upset over problems they've experienced in the past. A person who seems angry all the time because they think they have been treated unfairly or have a self-righteous feeling of oppression or inferiority. There was an American game in the 1800s that kids would play called 'chip on your shoulder' and it is also said to have been recorded when two boys were determined to fight. A chip of wood was placed on one's shoulder and the other had to knock it off. When the chip was knocked off, the fight began. Similar to Medieval times when a knight would throw down his gauntlet and if the opponent picked it up the challenge was accepted and the fight began. The chip is now a figure of speech, but the idea is the same.

Choc a block

Meaning: Passengers rammed in and have nowhere to move.

Origin: On the sailing ships of days gone by, blocks of rigging tackle would often tangle with each other and become tightly

fixed together. At sea this was known as 'choc a block' and the
expression passed from there into wider English usage to describe
any tightly packed situation.

Clog up

Meaning: To become obstructed.

Origin: 'Clog up the works' could have derived from Luddite
Dutch workers throwing their clogs into machinery to wreck it.
The French for clog is *sabot* and that was how 'saboteur' derived.

Close but no cigar

Meaning: An act or event coming very close to succeeding but
not quite close enough; it is thought to come from the custom of
lighting a big cigar to celebrate a major success.

Origin: The wandering fairs and circuses touring 19th-century
America and entertaining people along the way and many
sideshows would offer the public the prize of a large Havana cigar
for winning such competitions as shooting the spots off a playing
card, or smacking a mallet against a pad to try to make a nail shoot
up the pole and ring a bell located at the very top.

Come apart at the seams

Meaning: To become upset and lose control.

Origin: A piece of cloth with a seam, being stretched so much that
the two pieces of cloth come apart and rip open, just like a person
who is under a lot of stress or extremely upset, will fall apart and
break down.

Cool as a cucumber

Meaning: Calm and collected even in the face of difficulties.

Origin: Despite sounding like a modern-day phrase, cool as a cucumber actually first appeared in John Gay's Poems, *New Song on New Similies*, in 1732: 'I...cool as a cucumber could see the rest of womankind.'

Copper-bottomed agreement

Meaning: An agreement or contract which is the safest and most reliable.

Origin: This is a nautical expression deriving from copper sheathing ship makers used to strengthen boats; this would protect a ship from damage.

Crack pot

Meaning: A crazy person; a crank.

Origin: Cracked: Cracked is itself a shortening of 'brain-cracked' (or 'cracked-brained'). 'Cracked' simply meant 'impaired'; 'faulty'. Pot: In the Middle-Ages, 'pot' was used to mean 'skull' or 'head'.

Crocodile tears

Meaning: To fake being upset or force tears that are inauthentic.

Origin: An ancient anecdote by Photios claimed that crocodiles weep in order to lure prey. A crocodile when it eats, sheds the saline or salt as tears.

Cry havoc and let slip the dogs of war

Meaning: The military order, Havoc.

Origin: It was a signal given to the English military forces in the Middle Ages to direct the soldiery (in Shakespeare's parlance 'the dogs of war') to pillage and chaos. Shakespeare was well aware of the use of the meaning of havoc and he used 'cry havoc' in several of his plays. The 'cry havoc, and let slip the dogs of war' form of the phrase is from his *Julius Caesar*, 1601.

Cut of someone's jib

Meaning: To dislike how they look or what you hear about them.

Origin: This phrase was used at sea and was in common use by 1823. In naval terms the 'cut of its jib' refers to the overall condition of a sailing ship.

Cut it out

Meaning: Stop doing something bad.

Origin: It refers to getting a knife and start dissecting.

D

Darkside

Meaning: The evil and malevolent aspect of human personality or society often referred to in a lighthearted or comic context.

Origin: The wide adoption of the term 'The Dark Side' certainly came about as a result of the plotline of the 1977 film *Star Wars Episode IV: A New Hope*, written and directed by George Lucas. In that context, Lucas portrayed the 'dark side' concept as the evil aspect of the underlying controlling power of the Universe — which he called 'The Force'.

Davy Jones' locker

Meaning: The bottom of the sea; the resting place of drowned mariners.

Origin: Davy Jones is the evil spirit of the sea.

Dead ringer

Meaning: Somebody who looks just like another.

Origin: In medieval Britain, the medical profession was not quite as refined as it is now, and people could be pronounced dead, when they may have simply been unconscious. (And this was also before comas were fully understood.) It was not uncommon for bodies to be later exhumed by body snatchers, and corpses might be found with their fingers worn to the bone, a clear indication they had returned to life and tried to claw their way out of their coffins.

Dead wood

Meaning: A derogatory term given to that part of a working group that was not up to the standards of others.

Origin: The original 'dead wood' in a ship is the timber secured in a keel, which has no purpose at all other than to add weight and strength.

Devil and the deep blue sea

Meaning: To be caught between two equally bad situations.

Origin: On board the traditional wooden ships, sailors would regularly have to seal the seams between the planks with hot tar to prevent them from leaking. The 'devil' seam was the highest one adjacent to the waterways (or gutters) closest to the side of the ship. This was the longest seam on a boat and the most prone to leaking, so inevitably needed the most attention. In heavy seas or during battle, a sailor may slip, or be knocked, into the seam and find himself trapped halfway down the side of the ship, between the devil seam and the 'deep blue sea'.

Diehard

Meaning: Refers to someone with a strong dedication to a particular set of beliefs.

Origin: In the 1700s, the expression described condemned men who struggled the longest when they were executed by hanging. The phrase later became even more popular after 1811's Battle of Albuera during the Napoleonic Wars. In the midst of the fight, a wounded British officer named William Inglis supposedly urged his unit forward by bellowing, 'Stand your ground and die hard … make the enemy pay dear for each of us!' Inglis' 57th Regiment suffered 75 per cent casualties during the battle, and went on to earn the nickname 'the Die Hards'.

Dog days

Meaning: Very hot days during July and August.

Origin: The ancient Romans noticed that the hottest days of the year, that is, in late July and early August, coincided with the appearance of Sirius—the Dog Star, in the same part of the sky as the Sun. Sirius is the largest and brightest star in the *Canis Major* constellation, in fact it is the brightest star in the sky. The ancients believed that the star contributed to the heat of the day.

Don't throw the baby out with the bathwater

Meaning: Don't discard something valuable along with something undesirable.

Origin: In medieval times people shared scarce bathwater and by the time that the baby was bathed the water was so murky that the baby was in danger of being thrown out unseen.

Donkey's years

Meaning: A very long time.

Origin: The change from donkey's ears (supposed to be long) to donkey's years was no doubt aided by the belief that donkeys live a long time.

Double whammy

Meaning: A double blow or setback.

Origin: A whammy was originally an evil influence. It originated in the USA in the 1940s and is associated with a variety of sports.

Don't look a gift horse in the mouth

Meaning: Assessing the value of a gift

Origin: Horses' gums recede with age, leading to longer teeth. A common way to inspect a horse's 'worth' is to check its mouth, hence the phrase. Receiving a horse as a gift and immediately inspecting its value was considered offensive, much like inquiring about the worth of a present today is rude.

Don't count your chickens before they're hatched

Meaning: Don't be sure of the result even before you have done anything.

Origin: Aesop said it. He wrote of a young milkmaid balancing a pail on her head. The girl thought, 'The milk in this pail will provide me with cream, which I will make into butter, which I will sell in the market, and buy a dozen eggs, which will hatch into chickens, which will lay more eggs, and soon I shall have a large poultry yard. I'll sell some of the fowls and buy myself a handsome new gown and go to the fair, and when the young fellows try to make love to me, I'll toss my head and pass them by.' At that moment, the girl tossed her head and lost the pail of milk. Her mother admonished, 'Do not count your chickens before they are hatched.'

Don't give a jot or a tittle

Meaning: This implies a person cares nothing at all about something.

Origin: The phrase 'I don't give a jot' is thousands of years old and is identical to 'I don't give one iota'. The origins for both can be found in the early Greek language. A 'jot' is the letter 'iota', the smallest in the Greek alphabet. It was used at the time to imply 'the least of anything' and that is how the phrase became widely used for not caring in the slightest.

Down in the dumps

Meaning: When we are feeling low in spirits and thinking that perhaps life is passing us by.

Origin: This is from the Dutch word *domp*, which can be translated as 'hazy' or 'doleful'.

Dressed to the nines

Meaning: To dress exceptionally well.

Origin: There's no concrete consensus on the origin of 'dressing to the nines,' but the most popular theory comes from the fact that the very best suits used a full nine yards of fabric.

Drinking at the last chance saloon

Meaning: Someone runs out of options and that now is the time to produce results, before it's too late.

Origin: The source of this expression is probably the old westerns where the Last Chance Saloon was the inn at the end of town, the final chance for cowboys, outlaws and rustlers to have a good drink before riding off into the remote, sun-drenched, dusty plain—and no doubt falling off and discovered later proposing marriage to a cactus plant.

Dr Livingstone

Meaning: To express comic surprise when chancing upon old friends in unexpected places.

Origin: Dr. David Livingstone (1813–73) was a Scottish missionary and explorer. Once, after a long period of travelling in Central Africa, he became cut off from the outside world and not a word was heard from him for many years. It is said that American newspaper owner Gordon Bennett paid for the American journalist Henry Morton Stanley to look for him, expecting the event to make headline news. The 27-year-old correspondent set off in 1869 and found the missionary two years later at Lake Tanganyika. It was there he uttered the now famous phrase 'Dr Livingstone, I presume?' The remark made headline news at the time.

Dropping like flies

Meaning: We know we are losing people at a rapid pace.

Origin: The expression derives from the popular children's fairy tale 'The Brave Little Tailor' by the Brothers Grimm. In the story, the main character, a tailor, kills seven flies with a cloth and then makes himself a belt to celebrate the needless slaughter. The belt, which is decorated with the words Seven at One Blow, sets off a chain of misunderstandings and adventures that lead to the tailor becoming king of the land.

Dull as dishwater

Meaning: To describe any person that was not dear, bright and interesting, like a fast-running stream or a babbling brook; the person seemed boring and as dull as a ditch full of stagnant water and mud.

Origin: 'As dull as ditchwater' was the phrase used at the time and it is easy to see how that has changed over the years, the comparison being made instead with dull and dirty dishwater after the washing-up has been done.

Dumdum bullet

Meaning: On impact, the soft-nosed shells would rip open and cause massive internal damage to its intended (human) target.

Origin: Dumdum bullets were first manufactured by the British at Dum Dum, India, are of advantage only in jungle warfare against primitive tribes, where the danger is of sudden rushes of large numbers at close quarters. They are not used in European warfare because they are inaccurate and tend to foul guns. If they offered an advantage, they would be used, regardless of any treaty. The expression 'dumdum' has since been affectionately applied to any other soft-nosed cartridge designed to leave its victim's insides, hanging in tatters.

E

Ear mark

Meaning: To set aside for a particular purpose.

Origin: In these days, in western countries at least, most farm animal's ears are fitted with metal tags, which include details of the animal's ownership, date of birth etc. Before the 1950s, when ear tags became commonplace, the ownership of stock like pigs and sheep was denoted by the clipping of the ears. This formed a permanent record and was an alternative to branding.

Eating crow

Meaning: To admit a fault or to be proved wrong after taking a strong position.

Origin: The Bible lists crow as unfit for eating, and along with buzzards and rats, it was actually illegal to eat crow in the Middle Ages. As such, it was notably humiliating to consume.

Eat my hat

Meaning: A display of confidence in a particular outcome; for example, 'That cricket team always loses. If they win this match

I'll eat my hat'.

Origin: Eating one's hat is, of course, something we wouldn't want to attempt in reality and the phrase is only used when the speaker is quite certain of the outcome of some event.

Eating humble pie

Meaning: To make an apology for some misdemeanour, usually having to accept humiliation in the process.

Origin: The expression dates back to the Middle Ages and the banquet that would be held after a hunt. During the feast, the Lord of the manor and his peers would be served the finest cuts of venison. But the entrails and offal, known at the time as 'umbles', would be baked into a pie and served to those of a lower standing or out of favour with the Lord.

Egg on

Meaning: To egg someone on is to encourage them and urge them forward.

Origin: The 'egg' of 'egg on' is a straightforward variant of 'edge', so to 'egg someone on' is to edge, or urge, them forward. Egg and edge both have the look and feel of Viking words and this first impression turns out to be correct, as they both derive from the Old Norse '*eddja*'.

End of the story

Meaning: The talking is over—there's no more to be said.

Origin: US origin.

Ends of the earth

Meaning: The furthest reaches of the land.

Origin: The phrase 'the ends of the earth' derives from the

Bible, *Zechariah 9:10*.

Entering the lion's den

Meaning: Facing a hostile situation, which will undoubtedly test your character and nerve before an outcome is decided.

Origin: The modern use of the phrase implies that such a task is undertaken voluntarily but not without caution. However, back in the days when the Romans had such fun throwing humans into a pit full of hungry lions to be torn to shreds in the name of entertainment, the idea had an entirely different sense, as thieves and murderers would be executed in this way.

Every cloud has a silver lining

Meaning: Every bad situation has some good aspect to it.

Origin: 'There's a silver lining to every cloud' was the form that the proverb was usually expressed in the Victorian era.

Even Stevens

Meaning: It has been divided up equally.

Origin: This could refer to the way a financial reward has been shared out. Jonathan Swift wrote in his *Journal to Stella* (1748), 'Now we are even, quoth Stephen, when he gave his wife six blows for one.' In England the slang word for coins was 'stevens'.

Excuse my French

Meaning: Please forgive my swearing.

Origin: A phrase used when someone who has used a swear-word attempts to pass it off as French.

F

Face the music

Meaning: Accept the unpleasant consequences of one's actions.

Origin: A commonly repeated assertion is that 'face the music' originated from the tradition of disgraced officers being 'drummed out' of their regiment.

Fag end

Meaning: The dregs.

Origin: Nothing to with smoking. In the textiles trade, the last part of the piece of cloth was made of coarser material than the rest and left hanging loose. It came to be known as the fag end, possibly as a corruption of *'flag'*, meaning 'hang down'.

Fair and square

Meaning: Honest and straightforward, especially of business dealings.

Origin: In the 16th century 'square' meant 'fair and honest'.

Fait and accompli

Meaning: An accomplished fact; an action which is completed before those affected by it are in a position to query or reverse it.

Origin: The literal translation into English of this French phrase is a fact realized or accomplished—what might these days be called a done deal.

Fall guy

Meaning: Criminal slang meaning 'arrest'.

Origin: Here 'fall' is used with the criminal slang meaning of 'arrest' or 'period in prison'.

Fast asleep

Meaning: Sound asleep.

Origin: The 'fast' in 'fast asleep' derives from the Old German 'fest', meaning 'stuck firmly'; 'not easily moveable' — as in 'stuck fast'. 'Asleep' derives from 'sleep' in the same way that nautical adverbs like 'aground' and 'astern' derive from 'ground' and 'stern'. To be 'fast asleep' was to be stuck firmly in sleep, analogous to a beached ship being 'fast aground'.

The female of the species is more deadly than the male

Meaning: When threatened the female species causes more harm than the male species.

Origin: This now famous phrase is a line from Jungle Book author Rudyard Kipling's poem 'The Female of the Species', published in 1911.
'When the Himalayan peasant meets the he-bear in his pride,
He shouts to scare the monster, who will often turn aside.
But the she-bear thus accosted rends the peasant tooth and nail.
For the female of the species is more deadly than the male.'

Filthy lucre

Meaning: Ill-gotten gains.

Origin: The word 'lucre' derives from the Latin word *lucrum*, meaning 'profit', 'gain', 'greed' or 'wealth' and other similar Greek words for 'stolen goods'. The 'filthy' part has just been added to reinforce the idea of 'dirty' (i.e. stolen) money.

Finger in every pie

Meaning: A person who has an interest in many things, especially to do with business; interfering meddler.

Origin: The expression has been in use for over four hundred years and is applied to anybody with wide and varied business interests.

First water

Meaning: Of the highest quality.

Origin: This is from the gem trade. The clarity of diamonds is assessed by their translucence; the more like water, the higher the quality.

Flogging a dead horse

Meaning: Flogging a dead horse is an idiom that means a particular request or line of conversation is already foreclosed or otherwise resolved, and any attempt to continue it is futile; or that to continue in any endeavour is a waste of time as the outcome is already decided.

Origin: Dating from the 17th century, a 'dead horse' was a term for work which a person had been paid for in advance (and already spent). The present meaning, in the phrase 'flog a dead horse', is quite different. This is a reference to something that is entirely pointless and cannot result in any productive end. The phrase, which is also sometimes expressed as 'beating a dead horse', appeared in print in 1859, in the report of a UK parliamentary debate involving Francis Wemyss-Charteris Douglas, eighth earl of Wemyss and sixth earl of March—who was better known as Lord Elcho.

Fly by the seat of your pants

Meaning: Rely on instinct rather than logic or knowledge.

Origin: This aviation term emerged in 1938 in US newspapers, to describe pilot Douglas Corrigan's (slightly perilous) flight from the USA to Ireland. Aircraft initially had few navigation aids and flying was accomplished by means of the pilot's judgment.

Fly off the handle

Meaning: Lose one's temper suddenly and unexpectedly.

Origin: Coined by American writer Thomas C Haliburton in 1843 (he also invented 'won't take no for answer' and 'ginger up'), this phrase was inspired by the way an axe-head will fly off its handle if loose.

Fool's errand

Meaning: A pointless undertaking.

Origin: The description 'fool' is now often used as a contemptuous insult, but in the Middle Ages it didn't have such negative connotations. A fool then was a naive simpleton but regarded with respect and even admiration—somewhat the way that 'the fool on the hill' is portrayed in The Beatles' song.

Fools rush in

Meaning: The rash or inexperienced will attempt things that wiser people are more cautious of.

Origin: This is a shortened line from English poet Alexander Pope's *An Essay on Criticism*, 1709: 'For Fools rush in where Angels fear to tread'. The 'fools' in question are literary critics—although fool did not have such negative connotations in the 18th century. At that time a fool wasn't a simpleton, lacking in intelligence, simply someone who had behaved foolishly.

Footloose and fancy free

Meaning: Single and able to enjoy oneself.

Origin: The 'foot' here is the bottom part of the sail on a boat; if this became detached from the boom, the lower half of the sail was regarded as 'footloose' as it flapped around aimlessly in the wind ('fancy free'). The expression has been in regular use since the 18ᵗʰ century to describe single people having fun (probably not at sea though).

Fore

Meaning: When the shout of 'fore' goes up on a golf course, everybody who hears it ducks for fear of receiving a golf ball in the back of their head.

Origin: The word is usually misunderstood as 'four' but the correct spelling leads us to the root of the expression. The word 'fore' especially in nautical parlance, has always meant something that is ahead, or in front. It has been prefixed to many other words over the years, giving us foremen, forearms, forerunners, forethought, foremost, foresee, foretell, forestall and others.

Forty winks

Meaning: A brief nap.

Origin: The origin of the phrase 'forty winks' can be traced back to 1571 when the Church of England introduced thirty-nine articles which clergymen of the church were required to accept before their ordination. It was thought that reading these catechisms was tedious and that their meaning could be missed. Thus after reading through the thirty-nine articles someone would take forty winks. From this point on, 'forty winks' has meant a brief nap.

Foul your own nest

Meaning: To spoil what you have established (in particular close relationships in family and business) and prejudice your interests in the process.

Origin: This expression is actually an old proverb, known for over a thousand years, that warns: 'It is a foul bird that defiles its own nest.' The moral of the saying derives from the observation that a bird will not excrete in its own nest and will also clean up the waste of its young.

G

Gadzooks

Meaning: an exclamation of surprise or annoyance; a euphemistic shortening of God's hooks (the nails on the cross).

Origin: This word brings comic strip superheroes to mind, but like gee whizz, it's another minced oath—meaning 'God's words', and first used in various 17th century plays.

Gammy leg

Meaning: Not sufficiently strong to carry their full weight—it is a lame leg.

Origin: The term we should be using, in fact, is 'game leg'. 'Game' derives from the Irish word *cam*, meaning 'crooked'. It has been in use for centuries, right up until the 1950s, when 'game' started being pronounced 'gammy', so resulting in our modern expression.

Gee whiz!

Meaning: Characterized by or causing naive astonishment or wonder.

Origin: First used in the late 19th century, gee whiz is actually shorthand (or a 'minced oath' in linguistic terms) for Jesus.

Get into a scrape

Meaning: To find yourself in an awkward and embarrassing situation as a result of your own carelessness.

Origin: 'Scrapes' are holes in the earth that a deer will habitually dig by using its forefeet. They can be up to 45 cm deep and anybody, either on foot or on horseback, might easily find themselves in a scrape which could result in injury.

Get one's goat

Meaning: Irritate.

Origin: It's a horse racing term. Nervous horses could be calmed down by placing a goat in the stall with them. Dastardly rival horse owners would sometimes steal, or 'get', these goats, thereby upsetting the horse and making it likely to lose the race.

Give a tinker's dam

Meaning: To express complete and abject lack of interest in a subject, believing it to be worthless.

Origin: This has nothing to do with the word 'damn' or 'damnation', as is sometimes believed. A tinker is a type of traveller or gypsy who used to roam the countryside in his caravan looking for casual work, often repairing old pots, pans and kettles in exchange for food and clothing. The tinker would plug a hole in a pan by surrounding it with a wall of clay, although he sometimes used bread for the purpose, and this was known as a 'dam'. Hot solder was then poured in and allowed to set, plugging the gap. Once this had gone hard, the tinker's dam would be broken off and thrown away as it was now useless, which is how the phrase became applied throughout the countryside to anything of absolutely no value or interest whatsoever.

Get the sack

Meaning: Dismissal from employment.

Origin: This slang term for getting fired originates in France, and alludes to tradesmen, who would take their own bag or 'sac' of tools with them when dismissed from employment.

Given the cold shoulder

Meaning: When you are not welcome any more.

Origin: This phrase can be traced to the great banquets of medieval England. During the feasts, which usually lasted for days, sometimes even weeks, the host (perhaps an English lord or a prominent knight) would provide sumptuous meals of venison, beef, game and trout. All this would then be washed down with copious amounts of wine and ale while travelling musicians, dancers and jesters would entertain a gathering of noblemen and women, and possibly royalty too. It was customary at the time for the host to signal the end of the festivities by asking his cooks to serve slices from shoulders of cold beef, mutton or pork. It was regarded as far more in keeping with his status to send the message in that way rather than for him to visit all his many guests in person (sometimes in their hundreds) to inform them the party was over. These days to be 'given the cold shoulder' is perceived as rude and unkind, although in medieval times it was regarded as a civilized and polite gesture.

Given the seal of approval

Meaning: A project or an activity has been checked and given the go-ahead by those in authority.

Origin: Seals, whether of wood, bone or metal, have been used to authenticate documents for over two thousand years, pressed into a variety of materials, including clay, mud and wax. The coat of arms of an individual or official body, such as the government or the army, used to be engraved on to a signet ring, and this would then be pressed into the wax, sealing a document closed. The idea was to show the person on the receiving end that they were in receipt of a genuine, official document. Any document with the king's seal pressed into the wax was to be taken very seriously indeed, especially if the seal had also been made under the last line, indicating the proposal outlined in the document had been fully approved. The practice still continues to this day, although officials now use a rubber stamp to approve papers.

Given the mitten

Meaning: To be dismissed from your place of work or from an elected position.

Origin: The phrase was widely used between the 19th and 20th centuries although it has largely been replaced now by 'being fired' or 'given the sack'. A practice that began in the late 1500s consisted of a notice of dismissal being sent to a person in the form of a *'mittimus'*. The word derives from the Latin verb *mittere*, meaning 'to send (away)'.

Note: Prior to the invention of toolboxes, all English crafts- and tradesmen carried their tools around in a sack. Hence to be given the sack (in the sense of the sack being 'given back' to you) meant being discharged from employment, the worker either carrying his tools home or on to his next job.

Go berserk

Meaning: Behave in a frenzied and violent manner.

Origin: This term has something in common with 'run amok'. In Viking (Norse) origin a *'Berserker'* was a warrior of great strength and courage, who fought with wild ferocity. The word is believed to be derived from *'bear sark'*, that is, bear coat. That berserker fighting tradition, in which the warriors took on the spirit (or even in their belief, the shape) of bears whilst foaming at the mouth and gnawing the edges of their shields, is the source of the Vikings' fierce reputation.

Going cold turkey

Meaning: This is often considered to be the best way to wean a person off hard drugs, although the expression can also be applied to indicate how a person may feel in the absence of anything, from alcohol to chocolate and other foods that one might have to abstain from for dietary or health reasons.

Origin: The original idea was that a person withdrawing from using drugs would find their skin turning hard to the touch and translucent to look at, with goose pimples all over like the skin of a plucked turkey.

Going at full tilt

Meaning: To be performing something at top speed, whether sailing, running, riding, driving, etc., or it could refer to machinery operating as fast as it will possibly go.

Origin: In medieval England, jousting was known as 'tilting' and knights on horseback would charge at each other at high speed, lances aimed at their opponents. The phrase derives from the old English word *tealt*, which means 'unstable' or 'leaning'.

Go down like a lead balloon

Meaning: A poorly received speech, proposal or joke; be considered a flop by the public.

Origin: The US version of this phrase 'Go over like a lead balloon', first appeared in a Mom-N-Pop cartoon in several newspapers in 1924. It then fell out of use until after WWII—and was said to inspire a certain heavy metal band to name themselves Led Zeppelin.

Go the whole nine yards

Meaning: To try one's best.

Origin: World War II fighter pilots received a nine-yard chain of ammunition. Therefore, when a pilot used all of his ammunition on one target, he gave it 'the whole nine yards'.

Going hell for leather

Meaning: One is going as fast as one possibly can, usually in a clumsy and uncontrolled manner.

Origin: When riding as fast as this, a horseman was certainly putting a lot of wear into his leather saddle, thereby 'exchanging hell for leather'.

Go tell it to the marines

Meaning: A response to an unbelievable story or suggestion.

Origin: The phrase originated in England when the marines were considered inferior to regular soldiers and sailors as they worked on both land and sea and so were regarded by many as expert at neither, therefore stupid.

Go like biglio

Meaning: Operating at full speed and gusto.

Origin: This expression began to be used widely during the 19th century. It has a reference to Nino Biglio, who was a lieutenant under Garibaldi. He would race into battle and fight fearlessly; hence the phrase 'to fight like Biglio' was regularly used at the time.

Gone haywire

Meaning: In a mess.

Origin: In frontier towns of the United States, wire would be taken from hay bales and used for domestic jobs, such as hanging clothes or binding the stove together. A 'haywire' camp was one that was poor, backward, or slovenly.

Gone for a burton

Meaning: Indicates somebody has had an unfortunate mishap or that something or someone has been lost altogether.

Origin: Before the Second World War, Burton's Ales ran an advert depicting a football team with one player missing from the line-up, leaving a gap in the team photograph. The caption explained that the player had 'gone for a Burton'. This slogan was picked up by the RAF during the war and used as slang for a missing pilot who invariably had crashed in action into the sea (or 'the drink') and was affectionately referred to as having 'gone for a Burton'. He would be missing from the photographs in future.

Goody two shoes

Meaning: Someone who thinks they are perfect.

Origin: In the 1700s there was a nursery tale called '*The History of Little Good Shoes.*' The name 'goody two shoes' was given to a poor orphan named Margery Mean Well. She was so poor that she only owned one shoe. She was given a pair of shoes by a rich gentleman and was so happy that she kept repeating to everyone that she had two shoes. Around the turn of the 20th century, people who were considered self righteous were called goody goodies.

Gordon Bennett

Meaning: An expression of surprise and even respect.

Origin: James Gordon Bennett II was born in America in 1841, the son of Gordon Bennett, the founder of the New York Herald. With cash to spare, he lived a charmed life and when he eventually inherited his father's newspaper empire, began a spending spree. Gordon Bennett junior was a flamboyant character who enjoyed encouraging the innovative and exciting, such as the first-ever airplane race, the Gordon Bennett Cup, which was won by Glenn Curtis in 1909. He sponsored a balloon race in France, as well as yacht races, boxing championships, steam engine trials and car races. For his own part, Bennett was an extraordinary character who once flew a plane through an open barn as a stunt, burned a bulky roll of cash, which was in his back pocket causing discomfort, and urinated in his future in-laws' fireplace, in front of other guests, after drunkenly mistaking it for a toilet.

Grasp the nettle

Meaning: To face a difficult situation positively and with confidence.

Origin: Stinging nettles are painful when brushed against and can bring a person out in a nasty rash, but for centuries they have been known for their healing and nutritional value.

Graveyard shift

Meaning: The time a person works when the workplace is at its quietest.

Origin: The phrase was used widely during the Second World War when it was applied to the nightshift workers in the munitions factories. Since then, the phrase has been applied to other trades and professions. Journalists and news broadcasters have a 'graveyard shift', for example, which is often simply manning the phones overnight should any big news story break.

Gravy train

Meaning: A job that pays well for little work.

Origin: In the 1920s, gravy was a slang word for easy money usually gotten by illegal means. Gravy is a rich food and sometimes used to describe luxuries; to have it easy by making a living with little effort. During America's railroad days, the gravy train evolved when a 'gravy' run was an easy one with little work. To ride the 'gravy train' means to acquire an ongoing situation that provides good pay or other benefits with little labour or trouble. It may have come from those who hopped trains as a way of life. A train ride is an easy relaxing way of travel taking you where you want to go.

Green-eyed monster

Meaning: Jealousy personified.

Origin: Shakespeare coined this term in *The Merchant of Venice*, when Portia says: 'And shuddering fear, and green-eyed jealousy! O love, Be moderate;'. He then used green eyed monster again in his most famous play about jealousy—*Othello*.

Guns spiked

Meaning: To have one's plans foiled.

Origin: The earliest type of battlefield cannon was muzzle loaded and the only way it could be fired was by igniting gunpowder through a small charge-hole. In a simple but effective piece of military disruption, an enemy could put a gun out of action for a long time, sometimes even permanently, by driving a small metal spike deep into the charge-hole, which would seal it completely. It was a tricky job for a blacksmith to remove it and consequently just a handful of undercover agents could neutralize many of an army's guns in a very short time by using this method of sabotage. These days you are more likely to find it is your drink that is 'spiked', although in a different way and for different reasons.

H

Hair of the dog that bit you

Meaning: A small measure of drink, intended to cure a hangover.

Origin: This comes from the medieval belief, when someone was bitten by a rabid dog, a cure could be made by applying the same dog's hair to the infected wound. The symptoms of hangover are partly induced by a withdrawal from alcohol poisoning. A small measure of alcohol may be some temporary relief, even if in the longer term it makes the hangover worse.

Halcyon days

Meaning: Sun-filled, peaceful times that we look back upon with affection and nostalgia.

Origin: Halcyon is the Greek word for 'kingfisher' coming from the word *hals*, meaning 'the sea', and *kuon*, translated as 'to conceive and deriving in turn from the myth of the goddess Halkuon (or Halcyone)', who collapsed in grief when her husband was drowned in a shipwreck. It was said that when the news of the tragedy reached her, she threw herself into the sea and also drowned. The gods were so touched by her romantic gesture that they brought them both back to life as kingfishers, who lived happily ever after on a floating nest. The gods also decreed that from that time onwards whenever the kingfishers were breeding in their sea nests, which was always during the 14-day period of the winter solstice, the waters would be kept calm and the wind still. They were the calm and tranquil winter days that became known as 'halcyon days'.

Half-assed fashion

Meaning: Not concentrating fully or putting much thought or effort into it.

Origin: The original expression was *half adze*. An *adze* was, and still is, an axe-like tool with a curved blade that was used by carpenters to shape wood. The story goes that if you were wealthy and could afford to pay for fine furniture, you would buy pieces that had been finished completely, including the back and other unseen areas, such as inside drawers. However, if you were buying economically, you were likely to find all the unseen areas, such as those placed next to a wall, were unfinished and plain. These cheaper jobs were known as 'half adze' work.

Half-baked

Meaning: This is a similar expression as 'half-assed fashion.'

Origin: If an idea has not been thought through completely, it might be likened to bread that has not been sufficiently baked through and needs to be finished off. To avoid association with the undesirable term, bakers now produce 'part-baked' bread, instead of the original 'half-baked', meaning customers can go home and finish it off themselves.

Have a dekko

Meaning: Have a look.

Origin: This a word from the Raj days in India. 'Dekko' is the usual spelling; sometimes 'decko', sometimes 'deko'. The proper spelling, which is virtually never used, is *dekho*. The word is like a few others is from the British army harvested during the period of governance of India known as the British Raj (1858–1947).

Have another string to your bow

Meaning: Having more than one skill or opportunity and not to limit oneself to just one possible course of action.

Origin: This expression dates to the Middle Ages when archers would carry a second string attached to the top of their bows and wound around the handle. This meant that if their bowstring snapped, they were able to re-string the bow using the reserve bow string, so that they were always able to defend themselves or to continue hunting.

Having a yen for something

Meaning: A great desire or longing.

Origin: This is an American phrase. The yen in question is surprisingly not the Japanese currency, but a reference to Chinese opium, a drug freely available in both Britain and America during the late 1800s. The phrase comes from the Chinese word *yan*, which can be translated as craving.

Have no truck

Meaning: To avoid a person completely and have no dealings at all.

Origin: The root of this expression is Old French word *troquer*, meaning 'to barter'.

Head over heels

Meaning: Excited in love.

Origin: 'Head over heels' is now most often used as part of 'head over heels in love'. When first coined it wasn't used that way though and referred exclusively to being temporarily the wrong way up.

Heavens to Betsy

Meaning: Amazement, disbelief or astonishment.

Origin: It is thought to have originated in the United States during the alcohol prohibition era and used the same way we do today being one of the many non-curses to express amazement.

Heavy metal

Meaning: Hard rock music, usually electric guitar-based and always loud.

Origin: 'Heavy metal' seems at first a strange label to apply to a form of music. 'Heavy' was coined in the beatnik era of the 1950s to mean serious or profound and the term 'heavy music' was then and later applied to music in that vein. The word 'heavy' is derived from the usual meaning, that is, 'weighty or massive'.

Heebie jeebies

Meaning: In a state of high anxiety and fear.

Origin: This expression has a racial overtone and is in some way connected to the anti-Semitic word *Hebe* a derogatory term for 'Hebrew' (i.e. a Jew). However, nothing could be further from the truth. The source of this phrase lies in fact in the work of the popular American cartoonist William (Billy) De Beck, where it was used to mean 'the frights'.

Hell hath no fury like a woman scorned

Meaning: Indicates a woman, when deceived by her lover, will be so incensed that she'll do anything to get her own back, however violent or destructive.

Origin: The full line comes from William Congreve's play *The Mourning Bride* (1607): 'Heaven has no rage, like love to hatred turned, Nor hell a fury, like a woman scorned.'

High jinks

Meaning: To be lively and excited—basically having a good time.

Origin: This term has a Scottish origin. During this time there was a popular game where dice were thrown to see who among the group would have to drink a huge and potent cocktail which was likely to have the loser ricocheting along the corridors in no time at all. Then the dice would be thrown again and the loser this time would pay for the drink.

Hillbilly

Meaning: A 'fellow'.

Origin: The word first appeared in the 1900s. A hillbilly is a person who lives freely in rural areas of the South, often in the Appalachian Mountains and is isolated and a bit out of touch with modern culture. A hillbilly is stereotyped as a person who is a white southerner that goes barefoot, carries a shotgun, wears a worn out hat and clothes, has a long beard, bad teeth, is poorly educated, drinks moonshine whiskey, plays the banjo or fiddle and drives an old pickup truck.

Hit below the belt

Meaning: A remark that is a little offensive, insensitive and not in keeping with the spirit of matters.

Origin: In 1867, the Marquis of Queensberry produced a set of rules to govern the sport of boxing, as prior to this 'professional' fights were nothing more than a lawless brawl. One of the rules Queensberry introduced was that 'no boxer must ever aim a blow at an opponent below the level of his trouser belt'. If a boxer did so then that would be considered an unsporting gesture and the victim would be given 'as much time as he needs to recover'.

Hobson's choice

Meaning: No real choice at all—the only options being to either accept or refuse the offer that is given to you.

Origin: There is a story that this expression comes from a Mr Hobson who hired out horses and gave his customers no choice as to which horse they could take.

Hocus pocus

Meaning: Magical and misleading.

Origin: The magical phrase is probably a bastardization of the Roman Catholic liturgy of the Eucharist, which contains the phrase 'Hoc est corpus meum.'

Holding the purse strings

Meaning: One in control of the budget and financial spending

Origin: Originally, purses were leather pouches drawn closed at the top by a string. This was often then hung around a person's neck or tied to a belt around the waist. The person who had the money pouch tied to them was, quite literally, holding the purse strings.

Honeymoon

Meaning: This is the holiday that newly married couples take directly after their wedding. The expression is also applied to the period a person is given to settle into a new job or role before they are expected to produce positive results.

Origin: In ancient Egypt it was customary for a bride's father to provide his new son-in-law with all the mead he could drink for the period of one month. Mead is a type of wine made from honey and so that month (the period between one full moon and the next) was called the 'honeymoon' (literally 'honey month') in Europe. It was an ancient custom for all newly married couples to share a drink of diluted honey, during the first month of their marriage, to reinforce the 'sweetness' of those early weeks together.

A hooker

Meaning: A term applied to describe a prostitute.

Origin: There is a location in New York called Corlear's Hook, known locally as 'The Hook', which was a place where ladies of the night could apply their skills in the latter part of the 19th century. Another origin might be from a General Joseph Hooker. During the American Civil War, a certain area of Washington DC became known as 'Hooker's Division'.

I

In the doghouse

Meaning: The expression is traditionally applied to a husband, or male partner, who is unable to behave himself and is held in disgrace.

Origin: The source of this expression is found in J.M. Barrie's *Peter Pan* (1904) and the character Mr Darling, who is made to live in the dog kennel by his wife as a result of his behavior towards 'Nana'. He is only allowed to return to the house when his children return from Neverland.

In the doldrums

Meaning: In low spirits; feeling dull and drowsy.

Origin: The Doldrums is the region of calm winds, centered slightly north of the equator and between the two belts of trade winds, which meet there and neutralize each other. It is widely assumed that the phrase 'in the doldrums' is derived from the name of this region. Actually, it's the other way about. In the 19th century, 'doldrum' was a word meaning 'dullard; a dull or sluggish fellow' and this probably derived from 'dol', meaning 'dull' with its form taken from 'tantrum'.

In the limelight

Meaning: The center of attention.

Origin: Beginning in the 1840s, the lighting in theaters was a beam created by heating lime, a form of calcium oxide. A strong lens then directed this brilliant white light onto a solo performer on stage. The figurative use of someone or something being the center of attention outside the world of theater began around the turn of the 20th century.

In the offing

Meaning: Imminent; likely to happen soon.

Origin: This is one of the many phrases of nautical origin. It is quite simple to understand once you know that 'the offing' is the part of the sea that can be seen from land, excluding those parts that are near the shore. Early texts also refer to it as 'offen' or 'offin'. Someone who was watching out for a ship to arrive would first see it approaching when it was 'in the offing' and expected to dock before the next tide. The phrase has come from its naval origin into general use in the language and is now used to describe any event that is imminent. 'The offing', although more usually used in the context of ships arriving, derives from the adjective 'off', which was used since at least the 14th century to mean 'away from'—as in 'casting off', 'setting off', 'be off with you' etc.

In the same boat

Meaning: Experiencing the same situation or condition as someone else.

Origin: It was first used by the ancient Greeks. This expression refers to the risks that are shared by all the passengers in a small boat at sea. Over the centuries the meaning came to include all people in similar, unpleasant circumstances on land, sea or in the air.

Iron rations

Meaning: Emergency supplies usually to be carried about the person.

Origin: Originally the phrase indicated military rations made up principally of tinned food, but more recently it has been applied to any basic food that is easy to prepare and consume, carried by mountaineers, cyclists and other travellers or sportsmen and women.

It's a funny old world

Meaning: An acceptance of a situation, albeit reluctantly, but it can also be used to express an unexpected stroke of good fortune.

Origin: It is a phrase lifted directly from the film world and in particular the movie *You Are Telling Me* (1934), starring W.C. Fields. At one point the great man states: 'It's a funny old world, a man is lucky if he gets out of it alive.' The tongue-in- cheek humor of the line was enough for it to be repeated all over the land as soon as the film was released and become established as part of the English language.

I wouldn't touch it with a barge pole

Meaning: This is an expression we use when we want to keep something, or even a person, as far from us as possible, certainly further than arm's length.

Origin: The 'barge pole' is a relatively new addition to the idiom; originally 'tongs' was used instead of 'barge pole'. Charles Dickens popularized that phrase in *Hard Times* (1854): 'I was so ragged and dirty you wouldn't have touched me with a pair of tongs.'

J

Jack in the box

Meaning: A toy consisting of a box containing a figure with a spring, which leaps up when the lid is raised.

Origin: A jack-in-the-box is a harmless and amusing children's toy. 'Jack' is usually a clown figure, which pops up on a coiled spring when the box lid is opened.

Jack the lad

Meaning: A Jack the lad is known to be carefree, bold and perhaps a little troublesome at times, although generally popular with his peers.

Origin: The original 'lad' was Jack Sheppard, the 22-year-old son of an English carpenter born in London's Spital Fields area in 1702. His criminal antics made him notorious throughout England and he eventually became the subject of numerous plays and popular ballads of the time. He was repeatedly arrested and even imprisoned on four occasions and each time managed to effect a spectacular escape despite once being manacled to the floor and in solitary confinement. He escaped from St Giles' prison by sawing through the wooden ceiling and making his way across the roof tops of nearby houses, and he managed to pick the locks of his manacles using only his finger nail, then climbed a chimney to freedom. Such daring deeds captured the public imagination and he became something of a hero among ruffians.

Jam tomorrow

Meaning: Some pleasant event in the future, which is never likely to materialize.

Origin: This is from Lewis Carroll's *Through the Looking Glass and What Alice Found There*, 1871, in which the White Queen offers Alice 'jam tomorrow.'

Janus faced

Meaning: A hypocritical person.

Origin: Janus was a Roman deity who, myth tells us, was responsible for the gates of heaven (his name deriving from the word for 'gate'—*ianua*). He had two faces, one in the usual position, like yours and mine, and one at the back of his head, enabling him to see in all directions at once. The inference was that Janus could see all sides of a situation, and was able to agree with each argument in turn. All hypocritical people are to this day regarded as Two-Faced (like Janus). Janus has also given us the name for the month of January, a time of year that, like the god, looks in two directions—back to the Old Year and forward to the New.

Jaywalker

Meaning: One who crosses the street in a reckless or illegal manner.

Origin: Jay birds that traveled outside of the forest into urban areas often became utterly confused as they were unaware of the potential dangers in the city—like traffic. Amused by their erratic behavior, people used 'jaywalker' to describe someone who crossed the street irresponsibly.

John Hancock

Meaning: A term for signing an autograph.

Origin: John Hancock was a prominent Boston merchant whose signature, as president of the Continental Congress, appears as one of the first on the American Declaration of Independence of 1776. The signature is also by far the largest, and legend has it that Hancock, while adding his name to the document, commented: 'There—I guess King George or John Bull will be able to read that without his spectacles.'

Joined at the hips

Meaning: Inextricably linked; inseparable.

Origin: The evocative expression 'joined at the hip' derives from the situation of conjoined twins.

Jot a little

Meaning: A tiny amount.

Origin: A jot is the name of the least letter of an alphabet or the smallest part of a piece of writing. It is the Anglicized version of the Greek *iota*—the smallest letter of the Greek alphabet, which corresponds to the Roman 'i'.

Jumping the gun

Meaning: To have started a task too soon, before others were considered ready.

Origin: Often thought to have emerged in the field of athletics, where events begin at the sound of a starting pistol, the idiom may in fact be military in origin. On the battlefield, the artillery would be placed at the front of the army with the infantry waiting behind them for the order to be given to attack the enemy on foot. However, some ill-disciplined troops would quite literally jump over the guns and attack before being ordered to do so.

Jump on the bandwagon

Meaning: To join others and become part of the newest activity going on.

Origin: A bandwagon is a wagon that carries a band in a parade, political event or circus. The word bandwagon was coined in the USA in the 19th century, as the name for the wagon that carried a circus band. This phrase appeared in American politics in 1848. It is said that a famous circus clown, Dan Rice, used his bandwagon and its music for a political campaign. Other politicians sought out seats on the bandwagon as the campaign became more successful, hoping to become associated with its success. Bandwagons became common in campaigns and to jump on the bandwagon began to be used as a derogatory term, pointing out that the people were associating themselves with the success, instead of what they associated themselves with.

Just in time

Meaning: A manufacturing/delivery process where a minimum of goods are kept in stock. Items are planned to arrive precisely at the time they are required for use or dispatch.

Origin: Just In Time, or JIT, was coined to name and describe a manufacturing processes developed by Toyota in Japan in the 1950s and which spread to the US and UK in the 1970s.

K

Keep a stiff upper lip

Meaning: Remain resolute and unemotional in the face of adversity, or even tragedy.

Origin: The phrase is similar to 'bite the bullet', 'keep your chin up', and 'keep you pecker up'. In 1963, P.G. Wodehouse published a novel called *Stiff Upper Lip, Jeeves*. 'Keep a stiff upper lip' is one of the many phrases in English that are used to give advice.

Keep mum

Meaning: Remain silent.

Origin: Nothing to do with mothers. It's derived from the German word for 'mumble', *mummeln*. Hundreds of years ago people played a dice game called *mumchance*, which was played in complete silence.

Keep the wolf from the door

Meaning: To find a way of warding off poverty, and hunger in particular.

Origin: Since ancient times, the wolf has been a symbol of starvation and destitution, and almost all fables and legends depict the wolf as desperate and ravenous.

Kicked the bucket

Meaning: Those who are no longer of this world, the deceased.

Origin: Refers to abattoirs and slaughterhouses where culled animals would be hung by the hind legs from an overhead beam, called a 'bucket', while blood drained from the carcass into a tin bucket below. Any twitching or spasms would result in the poor creature kicking one of the buckets.

Kith and kin

Meaning: This refers to either close relatives or respected, loyal and long-term friends.

Origin: Originally, the word 'kith' meant neighbors or friends while 'kin' indicated 'blood relatives'. It was in the 1920 that the expression became regularly used when John Galsworthy published his book *In Chancery* (1920), which included the line: 'Its depleted bins preserved the record of family festivity: all the marriages, births and deaths of his kith and kin.' However, today we usually regard only close relatives as 'kith and kin'. The Old English Word for 'kith' was *cythth*, meaning 'relationship', and the word used for 'kin' was *cynn*, which meant 'family'.

Knock seven bells

Meaning: To hand out a serious beating, but not actually knock the person unconscious.

Origin: This is a nautical term. The expression comes from the eight bells on board a ship. Hence to put only seven of them out of action meant to stop shy of making a complete job of it.

Knocked into a cocked hat

Meaning: When something, or someone, has been soundly defeated and proved to be inferior to another.

Origin: This is an American phrase connected to the headgear worn by Puritans in the 17th century. They wore their hats with the brim turned up (cocked) on three sides, giving their heads a strange triangular appearance that was ridiculed by many. It is said that comedians and jesters of the day would remove the hat of a fellow actor and knock it into a 'cocked hat shape' to show themselves to be dominant and superior, much to the delight of the crowds.

L

Lager louts

Meaning: Young people whose sole weekend ambition is to drink as much alcohol as they can, go to a football match and start a fight.

Origin: Such cultural pastimes became popular in Britain during the 1980s as employment began to rise and memories of the recession of the late 1970s blurred in a haze of hangovers.

Lame duck

Meaning: A person (or venture) with no influence and no future.

Origin: The expression has been used since 1761 and is said to have been applied to a defaulter on the London Stock Exchange who could not pay his debts and would have to 'waddle' out of Exchange alley in the City of London in disgrace.

Land lubber

Meaning: A person who is much happier on dry land than at sea (a phrase used by sailors).

Origin: The expression is not a corruption of 'land lover'. 'Lubber' was ship's language for a big, lumbering, clumsy novice. Adding the word 'land' only accentuates the insult.

Learn and inwardly digest

Meaning: Contemplation of a subject in order to learn from it.

Origin: The source of this expression is found in a prayer for the second Sunday of Advent, in *The Book of Common Prayer*: 'Grant that we may in such wise hear them, read, mark, learn and inwardly digest them.'

Left handed compliment

Meaning: A negative or abusive compliment.

Origin: This is one of those phrases where 'left-handed' is used in a negative or abusive way without any real reason. This expression uses left-handed in the sense of 'questionable or doubtful,' a usage dating from about 1600. Another explanation is that a left-handed compliment is an insult concealed in an apparent compliment and thus is the reverse of a real compliment, as left is the reverse of right. The left side has long been associated with wrongness and being 'sinister'.

Lightning never strikes twice

Meaning: To offer consolation to someone after a recent misfortune and to remind them it is unlikely ever to happen again.

Origin: It is an expression based on superstition, and one that might encourage us to tempt fate by doing something again in the belief that the same bad luck cannot repeat itself.

Let the cat out of the bag

Meaning: Divulge a secret.

Origin: In times gone by, farmers would bring suckling pigs to market wrapped up in a bag. Unscrupulous ones would substitute a cat for the pig. If someone let the cat out of the bag, the deceit was uncovered.

Let your hair down

Meaning: To relax or be at ease.

Origin: Parisian nobles risked condemnation from their peers if they appeared in public without an elaborate hairdo. Some of the more intricate styles required hours of work, so it was a relaxing ritual for these aristocrats to come home at the end of a long day and let their hair down.

Let bygones be bygones

Meaning: To forgive and forget without allowing past events to influence our attitude in the future.

Origin: This is a proverbial expression used in England since 1546, deriving from the Old English word *bygone*, meaning 'thing of the past'.

Lion's share

Meaning: The larger portion.

Origin: This is from Aesop's Fable dating to around 600 BC. The tale tells us how a lion, a fox and an ass went hunting and killed a stag, which the ass promptly divided into equal portions, but the lion looked upon this gesture as an insult to his pride and dignity, so he ate the ass. The fox was a little more cunning and ate just a small part, leaving the lion the largest share. The moral here is don't be an ass but be a little more fox-like and cunning instead.

However, it is also a fact that the lion does naturally get the largest share of any kill brought to him by one of the lionesses in a pride.

Life is just a bowl of cherries

Meaning: Everything that is wonderful with our lives is still a popular one, especially in the North of England.

Origin: It is a comparatively modern proverb, which originates from the musical *Scandals*, first produced in America in 1919, which included a popular song entitled 'Life is Just a Bowl of Cherries' by George Gershwin.

Loophole

Meaning: A small opening thorough which small arms are fired, to admit light and air, or for observation.

Origin: In the late Middle Ages, a loop was a narrow window in a castle that an archer could shoot through, but so narrow that it made it almost impossible for his enemy to shoot back through. This became the loophole. It is now used to mean an escape or omission in text to evade a contract or obligation.

M

Mad as a hatter

Meaning: Completely insane.

Origin: In the 19th century Mercury used to be used in the making of hats. This was known to have affected the nervous systems of hatters, causing them to tremble and appear insane. Mercury poisoning is still known today as 'Mad Hatter's disease'.

Make ends meet

Meaning: To live frugally.

Origin: The word 'meet' is an early accounting term meaning 'to match' or 'to balance'.

Make no bones about it

Meaning: To find no difficulties or problems with something and to speak directly, plainly, honestly without hesitation.

Origin: It dates back to the 14th or 15th century England when someone wanted to express their dissatisfaction with something. This saying is believed to be related to soup. It is a reference to the unwelcome discovery of bones in soup. Soups with bones in them were difficult to swallow, and the soups that were strained to remove the bones were not. If you found no bones in your meal you were able to swallow it without any difficulty or objection without worrying about choking. When you make no bones about something, people feel they can swallow or accept your answer.

Man after my own heart

Meaning: A kindred spirit—someone I can agree with.

Origin: This saying comes from the Bible (King James Version): Samuel 13:14: 'But now thy kingdom shall not continue: the Lord hath sought him a man after his own heart, and the Lord hath commanded him to be captain over his people, because thou hast not kept that which the Lord commanded thee.'

Masterpiece

Meaning: Any great work of art can be acknowledged as a masterpiece. The expression is not restricted just to the visual arts either and can be traced to the Netherlands, to around 1580.

Origin: Originally, a craftsman, artist, writer or musician would mark the end of their training period and apprenticeship by producing a work reflecting their new status as 'master of the guild'. This one piece of work was called the 'master piece' and the phrase has been applied to exceptional creations ever since.

Mealy-mouthed

Meaning: Unable to speak simply or directly.

Origin: It's an improper pronunciation of the Greek word *melimuthos*, meaning 'honeyed speech'.

Meet one's waterloo

Meaning: Suffer a comprehensive defeat after enjoying a run of great success.

Origin: By 1815, Napoleon Bonaparte had created an empire that incorporated nearly all of Europe. His battlefield successes between 1809 and 1811 had been complete and his military strategy was feared and respected across the continent, until 18 June, 1815, and the events that took place near the small town of Waterloo in Belgium. It was here that the Duke of Wellington and his allied forces, despite being heavily outnumbered, finally crushed Napoleon's army, sending the Napoleon into exile and captivity on the island of St Helena, where he died in 1821. The Battle of Waterloo ended 26 years of war between the major European powers and France (the Napoleonic Wars) and peace finally fell across the continent once again.

Men in grey suits

Meaning: These are the faceless bureaucrats or administrators who govern and control many aspects of our lives without proper accountability.

Origin: This expression was first used by the Beatle, John Lennon, when the world-famous band formed their own company, the

Apple Organization, in the 1960s. Lennon was quoted at the time as saying: 'This is an attempt to wrestle control from the men in suits.'

Mind your p's and q's

Meaning: To be extremely exact and be careful no to do or say anything wrong. It also means to mind your manners.

Origin: This saying started to be used in the 1600s and became very popular in the 1700s. It may have come from the fact that the letters p and q are often confused when a child learns to read and write as well as printers who choose these letters when selecting type. It also may have come from the old English pubs. They would list a the number of pints (p's) and quarts (q's) a person consumed on a blackboard to keep track of payment. There is also the use of the dance steps called pieds (p's) and queues (q's) that a French dancing instructor would use to teach his students.

Mob

Meaning: A crowd of people who usually have violent intentions.

Origin: This stems from the Latin phrase *mobile vulgus*, meaning 'unruly crowd'.

Moseying about

Meaning: Someone wandering around in an unhurried manner in search of something, perhaps in a bookshop or a craft market.

Origin: The early Spanish settlers to the New World introduced many words, including *vamos*, which may be translated as 'let's go' and is the origin of the word *vamoose* meaning 'to depart hurriedly'. The word 'mosey' is a corruption and slight extension of the Spanish word by English settlers.

Movers and shakers

Meaning: People of energetic demeanour who initiate change and influence events.

Origin: The expression 'movers and shakers' is now most often applied to the rich and powerful in politics and business. The original movers and shakers were used in board games like *Snakes and Ladders*; those have shaken dice, moves and winners and losers.

My ears are burning

Meaning: I can hear someone talking about me.

Origin: It goes back to the ancient Romans, who had a strange obsession with burning sensations in various organs. If your left ear tingled, it signaled evil intent from outside influences. If your right ear tingled, you were being praised or were in line for some good luck.

N

New kettle of fish

Meaning: 'Another matter altogether' or a 'different situation'.

Origin: The word 'kettle' in this case is a corruption of the Old English *kiddle* which was a grille set across a river to catch passing fish. A more likely origin can be found in the Scottish Border country where it was common for families and friends to spend the day feasting and socializing on the banks of a river. The main food of the day would be salmon, freshly caught in the river and cooked on a 'kettle' or barbecue. For this reason, the outings were known across Scotland as a 'kettle of fish'.

Nineteen to the dozen

Meaning: Going very fast.

Origin: In Cornish mines in the 18th century, pumps were installed to drain floodwater. When working at full capacity, they could drain 19,000 gallons of water for every 12 bushels of coal that powered them.

Nip something in the bud

Meaning: To deal with a problem in the early stages in order to prevent an escalation.

Origin: The expression has been around for five hundred years or so, and if it had been made clearer from the outset, hundreds of schoolboys would not have been in trouble for pruning a prized plant at around an inch from the ground when asked merely to nip it in the bud.

No dice

Meaning: There is no chance or probability of an event happening.

Origin: No dice is a 20th century American saying that comes from gambling games that use dice. It is used to show that there is no chance or probability of an event happening. Gamblers were very careful about hiding their dice when the police came around, since gambling with dice was illegal in many states. The dice was used as evidence of gambling in the courts. Some cases were even thrown out due to the absence of the dice, no dice, no conviction. In the game of Craps, when a throw is out of play or a die is not lying flat, the throw is not valid and is ruled as 'no dice'.

No holds barred

Meaning: No rules apply and any measures may be taken to ensure a favourable outcome.

Origin: This is a wrestling expression, similar to the 'gloves are off' in boxing, which also means that the rules of the sport are being disregarded on this occasion. In wrestling, certain holds are banned because they are considered too dangerous.

No quarter asked for and no quarter given

Meaning: No leniency is expected or will be given under any circumstances, usually in the business arena or on the sports field.

Origin: Originally the expression was used on the battlefield and, rather ominously, the word 'quarter' is the old English word for 'mercy'. A defeated army could possibly cry out for 'quarter' while surrendering, but usually pride and foolish bravery prevented them from doing so. Instead, they would accept any punishment meted out by their enemy. The expression can often be found in historic military records in reference to captured prisoners.

No spring chicken

Meaning: Someone who is past his prime.

Origin: New England chicken farmers generally sold chicken in the spring as they gave better returns than the chicken that survived the winter. Sometimes, farmers tried to sell old birds for the price of a new spring chicken. Seasoned buyers complained that the fowl was 'no spring chicken,' and so the term came to describe someone who was past his prime.

Nothing is certain except death and taxes

Meaning: Any event that could have more than one outcome; nothing is guaranteed in life.

Origin: Of American origin, the phrase is a direct quote from one of the founding fathers, whose signature appears on the Declaration of Independence—Benjamin Franklin no less. In 1789, political opponents were pressing Franklin for a prediction of how the new constitution would work for the American people. Within a week, part of Franklin's reply had made headlines all across the new country, and subsequently in Britain: 'Our Constitution is in actual operation and everything appears to promise that it will last; but in this world nothing is certain but death and taxes.'

Not to mince your words

Meaning: To speak plainly, frankly and with brutal honesty.

Origin: The phrase is always used in the negative sense. As the saying goes some things we are told are unpleasant and difficult to take in, and the allusion is drawn from butchers who mince cheaper cuts of meat, often full of bones and gristle, to make them easier to swallow and digest. It has always been felt that a person 'not mincing his/her words' is not making any effort to soften their impact.

O

Off the record

Meaning: Something that has not been officially recorded.

Origin: This American phrase was first attributed to President Franklin Roosevelt in 1932, who was recorded in The Daily Times-News saying 'he was going to talk 'off the record', that it was mighty nice to be able to talk 'off the record' for a change and that he hoped to be able to talk 'off the record' often in the future.'

Off to see a man about a dog

Meaning: When a person is not keen to tell us where they are going, they may instead remark they are 'off to see a man about a dog'.

Origin: During the age of the Victorian music hall and theatre, in a popular play called *Flying Scud* (1866) by Dion Boucicault, whenever the lead character found himself in an awkward situation, he would take his leave by announcing he 'had to see a man about a dog'. Audiences found this very funny, and people were soon copying the expression.

Once in a blue moon

Meaning: Very rare.

Origin: A blue moon is the second full moon in a single calendar month, and it's very rare. The phrase 'once in a blue moon' is used colloquially to mean something that doesn't happen very often.

On the right track

Meaning: A person following the correct procedure.

Origin: This is actually a corruption of 'to be on the right track', a nautical term. A sailing ship, heading into the wind, must plot a left-to-right, zig-zag type of path if it is to make progress. This type of coursing is known as 'tacking' and to 'go off on the wrong tack' will lead to a ship making very little progress.

On their high horse

Meaning: Those who appear dismissive and aloof, as if looking down upon the rest of us.

Origin: Medieval knights and other noblemen used to wear magnificent suits of armour, which would weigh around 300 pounds. As a result, they could only ride specially bred horses, which were much larger than normal and hence able to carry the extra weight. It was not uncommon for noble gentlemen to ride through English towns looking down upon the locals on their ordinary-sized nags. Later, politicians would parade in ceremonial processions mounted on outsized horses, leading to the expression 'he is up on his high horse again'.

On your beam ends

Meaning: To be virtually destitute; run out of cash and one had better start making other plans.

Origin: It is recorded that a ship known to be on its beam ends was listing so badly that it was said to be sailing virtually on its side. To be so close to capsizing completely, with such disastrous consequences, was no place to be at all, and neither is being virtually bankrupt—so the parallel was drawn.

Once the die has been cast

Meaning: A chain of events has been started and there is no turning back; the deed is irreversible.

Origin: The expression is credited to Julius Caesar, uttered when he sent his army across the Rubicon and into war with Rome.

Other side of the coin

Meaning: The opposite side or point of view of a situation.

Origin: It has been around since the 2oth century. Even though a coin has two sides, you can only see one side at a time. Issues like coins always have two sides. In order to get the full story, you need to hear both sides or the other side of the coin to get the whole story. There are two sides to every story.

Out like a light

Meaning: To fall asleep fast or suddenly become unconscious.

Origin: When the use of electricity started spreading in the 20th century, it became easier and faster for people to turn their lights on and off with the flick of a switch. It had now become so much faster to turn out the light that the saying 'out like a light' was used to refer to the quick action.

Over a barrel

Meaning: To be helpless, at a disadvantage or in a bad situation.

Origin: When a person was flogged or whipped for a crime, they were often tied over a barrel to hold them down. A person was laid over a barrel to help empty their lungs of water when they were rescued from drowning.

P

Paint the town red

Meaning: Wild and reveling enjoyment.

Origin: It owes its origin to one legendary night of drunkenness.
In 1837, the Marquis of Waterford — a known lush and mischief
maker — led a group of friends on a night of drinking through
the English town of Melton Mowbray. The bender culminated in
vandalism after Waterford and his fellow revelers knocked over
flowerpots, pulled knockers off of doors and broke the windows
of some of the town's buildings. To top it all off, the mob literally
painted a tollgate, the doors of several homes and a swan statue
with red paint. The Marquis and his pranksters later compensated
Melton for the damages, but their drunken escapade is likely the
reason that 'paint the town red' became shorthand for a wild night
out. Another theory suggests the phrase was actually born out of
the brothels of the American West, and referred to men behaving
as though their whole town were a red-light district.

Pass the buck

Meaning: Pass on responsibility.

Origin: In an old English card game, a jackknife, or 'buck', was
passed from player to player to indicate whose turn it was to play.

Play ducks and drakes

Meaning: To behave recklessly; to idly squander one's wealth.

Origin: Ducks and drakes is the old English name for the pastime
of skimming flat stones on the surface of water to make them
bounce as many times as possible.

Peters out

Meaning: Something that suddenly ended without notice or forewarning.

Origin: During the Californian gold rush of the mid-19th century, the explosive used to open up the seams in a gold mine was gunpowder, a combination of charcoal, sulphur and saltpetre or 'saltpeter' in US spelling—hence 'peter', and once a seam had been fully mined and exploited it was known to be 'petering out', which is how the expression became widely used in America and then crossed the Atlantic to Britain during the late 1800s.

Play devil's advocate

Meaning: To be in the position of presenting a hypothetical argument to a suggestion or proposal.

Origin: The source of this expression lies with the Catholic Church and the process of proposing a name for canonization, which is to make an individual into a saint. When a name is proposed, a member of the clergy is appointed to present the opposing argument and that person is known as the *advocatus diaboli*, from the Latin words *advocatus*, meaning 'summoned one', and *diaboli*, 'of the devil'. Thus the 'devil's advocate' has been summoned from the devil to present his argument.

Play the race card

Meaning: To attempt to gain advantage in an election by pandering to the electorate's racism. Also, more recently, to attempt to gain advantage by drawing attention to one's race.

Origin: This term is now more often used in the USA than in other countries. A 'race card' is the name of the card that lists the runners and riders at horse races, but that's not the race card being referred to in 'playing the race card'. The expression alludes to the trump card in card games like whist.

Pleased as punch

Meaning: To be very happy.

Origin: A 17th century puppet show for children called Punch and Judy featured a puppet named Punch who always killed people. The act of killing brought him pleasure, so he felt pleased with himself afterwards.

Picnic

Meaning: Social get-togethers with an outing.

Origin: In France at the time, a new type of party had been introduced known as a picnic, in which the guests would bring along a share of the food and wine so that the burden of providing would not be left to only one family. These social get-togethers were often held in outdoor public places, and to this day the word is used to describe an outdoor meal, usually with friends.

Pipe dreams

Meaning: An unrealistic hope or fantasy.

Origin: The allusion is to the dreams experienced by smokers of opium pipes. Opiates were widely used by the English literati in the 18th and 19th centuries.

Point of no return

Meaning: Impossible to go back, do something different or change your mind.

Origin: During WWII, pilots knew that they only had enough fuel to fly so many miles. When they reached the point of no return and had a shorter distance to go than if they turned back, they had to continue. Turning back at this point would mean running out of gas. It is also used when someone must continue on with a certain course of action that they have chosen, because turning back would be dangerous, expensive or physically impossible.

Poor as a church mouse

Meaning: Poverty-stricken or very poor. This saying was originally said to be 'hungry as a church mouse'.

Origin: Churches in the 1600s had no kitchens to cook meals and no storage or pantries to store food. A mouse that was so unlucky to take up residence in a church would find no food there. The lucky mice would find a place to live in the cellar of a house, restaurant or a grocery store, not a church. As time went on, the saying was changed from hungry to poor.

Pour oil on troubled waters

Meaning: To calm down a heated situation or to prevent an argument or a dispute from raging out of control.

Origin: The root of this expression can be found in a legend recalled by the Venerable Bede in his *Ecclesiastical History of the English People* (731). The story tells of a priest named Utta who was given the job of escorting King Oswy's bride across the sea. The weather looked troublesome and Utta was not keen on the task until approached by Bishop Aiden, who gave him a bottle of holy oil. The bishop had foreseen a storm at sea but reassured Utta that the oil would immediately calm the waters and make his journey safe and comfortable. As expected, a fierce storm did descend upon the boat, terrifying the king's bride and leaving all the sailors fearing for their lives. Utta remembered the bishop's words, found the bottle and poured the oil over the side. The sea was immediately calmed and everybody completed the voyage in safety. Since then, it has been the 'oil' of soothing language or actions that have calmed troubled waters of a figurative kind.

Propose a toast

Meaning: A friendly gesture towards the other guests present and wishing good fortune to all.

Origin: The origin can be traced to horse racing.

Punch

Meaning: A drink we are often served at picnics and it is one to be avoided at all costs. Some hosts delight in making a punch of the strongest alcohol available, which usually ends up tasting like it should be poured into the engine of a rusty tractor.

Origin: During the early 1600s, as English explorers first made their way to the Indian sub-continent, one of their discoveries was a popular drink that consisted of five ingredients: water, sugar, spirits, spices and fruit juice. The Hindi word for five is *punch* and this is how the drink became known when it was served back in England throughout the social gatherings of the day.

Pull out all the stops

Meaning: Achieve the maximum.

Origin: The 'stops' are knobs on an organ console. If the organist pulled them all out, he would be squeezing the most volume out of the instrument possible.

Put your shoulder to the wheel

Meaning: To add your effort to a joint task, as you will benefit in the long term.

Origin: This is an expression first recorded in 1692 and calls to mind the horse-drawn carriage. Before the invention of tarmac, it was common for a carriage to become stuck in the mud. When this happened, the driver would ask his passengers to help shift the carriage by disembarking and 'putting their shoulder to the wheel'. Royalty, nobility, gentry or otherwise, they would all have to lend a hand as there was no chance of the driver shifting it on his own.

Put up your dukes

Meaning: Put up your fists and prepare to fight.

Origin: The 'dukes' are the hands or fists. The use of 'dukes' meaning 'hands' is first referred to in print in the mid-19th century, in both England and the USA.

Q

Quality Assurance (QA)

Meaning: This is a way of preventing mistakes or defects in manufactured products and avoiding problems when delivering solutions or services to customers. QA is applied to physical products in pre-production to verify what will be made meets specifications and requirements.

Origin: During the Middle Ages, guilds adopted responsibility for quality control of their members, setting and maintaining certain standards for guild membership. Royal governments purchasing material were interested in quality control as customers. For this reason, King John of England appointed William Wrotham to report about the construction and repair of ships. Centuries later, Samuel Pepys, Secretary to the British Admiralty, appointed multiple such overseers. The Industrial Revolution led to a system in which large groups of people performing a specialized type of work were grouped together under the supervision of a foreman who was appointed to control the quality of work manufactured.

Quality time

Meaning: Time in which individual attention is given to an otherwise neglected child or partner.

Origin: From the 1970s, when the notion that parents could 'have it all', that is, a successful career and a happy home life, this term gained popularity.

Queer the pitch

Meaning: Interfere with or spoil the business of a tradesman or showman. (More recently) spoil the business at hand.

Origin: 'Queer' has been used as a verb meaning 'to spoil' since the early 19th century.

Quid pro quo

Meaning: Something given in return for a item of equivalent value—like tit for tat.

Origin: A Latin term meaning 'something for something' or 'this for that'.

Quiz

Meaning: Asking questions and finding answers.

Origin: Quiz nights in pubs and clubs throughout the world are as popular today as they ever have been, but to find the source of the word we must travel to Dublin. During the 1700s, a man called Daly was the manager of a theatre in the centre of the city. In 1780, he made a wager with friends one evening that he could introduce a brand new word, with no meaning at all, to the English language, and what's more he said he could do it within 48 hours. The bet was accepted and within hours Daly had chalked the letters Q-U-I-Z on doors and walls all over the city. The word immediately became the centre of attention and within weeks newspapers were running features on what it may possibly mean. Daly won his bet because the word became associated with asking questions and finding answers, with people mulling over the 'quiz' question in coffee houses and inns throughout Ireland and England.

R

Raining cats and dogs

Meaning: Raining heavily.

Origin: In Norse mythology, cats symbolized heavy rain, while dogs were associated with Odin the storm god, and therefore represented howling wind.

Read the riot act

Meaning: An Act read out to the public asking them to disperse and depart peacefully, especially after a riot.

Origin: These days, angry parents might threaten to 'read the riot act' to their unruly children. But in 18th-century England, the Riot Act was a very real document, and it was often recited aloud to angry mobs. Instituted in 1715, the Riot Act gave the British government the authority to label any group of more than 12 people a threat to the peace. In these circumstances, a public official would read a small portion of the Riot Act and order the people to 'disperse themselves, and peaceably depart to their habitations.' Anyone that remained after one hour was subject to arrest or removal by force. The law was later put to the test in 1819 during the infamous Peterloo Massacre, in which a cavalry unit attacked a large group of protestors after they appeared to ignore a reading of the Riot Act.

Red herring

Meaning: A distraction from the main issue.

Origin: It comes from fox hunting. A red herring has a strong odour. Hounds chasing a fox could be distracted by the smell of the herring and start following that instead.

Red-letter day

Meaning: A special or happy day.

Origin: In the 15th century, medieval church calendars and manuscripts wrote religious holiday, festivals and saints' days in red ink, while all other days were written in black ink. The red-letter days were the special ones.

Red tape

Meaning: Unnecessary official delay caused because of stringent or complex procedures for a bureaucratic approval.

Origin: Red ribbon was once used by government employees and lawyers to tie up bundles of legal documents. Before any official business could be done, the red tape had to be cut.

Resting on laurels

Meaning: Reaping the benefits of past good work.

Origin: The idea of resting on your laurels dates back to leaders and athletic stars of ancient Greece. In Hellenic times, laurel leaves were closely tied to Apollo, the god of music, prophecy and poetry. Apollo was usually depicted with a crown of laurel leaves, and the plant eventually became a symbol of status and achievement. Victorious athletes at the ancient Pythian Games received wreaths made of laurel branches, and the Romans later adopted the practice and presented wreaths to generals who won important battles. Venerable Greeks and Romans, or 'laureates', were thus able to 'rest on their laurels' by basking in the glory of past achievements. Only later did the phrase take on a negative connotation, and since the 1800s it has been used for those who are overly satisfied with past triumphs.

Right proper Charlie

Meaning: A harmless fool.

Origin: The full phrase starting out as a 'Charlie Smirke' rhyming slang for 'berk', the name of a successful English jockey who raced between the 1930S and 1950s. To call somebody a Berk is also generally regarded as an affectionate and humorous put down, lacking any malice.

Ringing the changes

Meaning: Someone in authority is announcing variation, which tends to result in matters being carried out in much the same way as before.

Origin: The source of this term can be found in the old English custom of bell ringing in the cathedrals and churches throughout the land. The 17th century brought about 'change ringing' ('changes' being the different order in which certain sets of bells can be rung).

Round Robin

Meaning: A document signed by multiple parties.

Origin: 'Robin' is a corruption of the French *ruban*, meaning ribbon. These petitions were originally signed in a circle so that no single person's name appeared at the top. The shape of the signatures resembled a circular ribbon.

Rooting for someone

Meaning: To be right behind everything they do and wanting them to succeed,

Origin: The expression originates from the sports stadiums where supporters would urge on their teams by singing, cheering and generally causing uproar. 'Rooting' for somebody could be a corruption of the phrase 'to rout', meaning to cause uproar.

Rubbing salt into the wound

Meaning: To make a person's shame, or pain in an emotional sense.

Origin: This is nautical in origin. Once an errant sailor had been punished by flogging, his comrades would rub preserving salt into his wounds, making them much more painful but healing the injuries a good deal faster than if they had been left untended.

Rub the wrong way

Meaning: To irritate, bother, or annoy someone.

Origin: In colonial America, servants were required to wet-rub and dry-rub the oak-board floors each week. When they rubbed it against the grain they caused streaks to form, making the wood look terrible and ending up irritating the homeowner.

Rule of the thumb

Meaning: A means of estimation made according to a rough and ready practical rule, not based on science or exact measurement.

Origin: The 'rule of thumb' has been said to derive from the belief that English law allowed a man to beat his wife with a stick so long as it is was no thicker than his thumb.

Running the whole gamut of emotions

Meaning: This is an unusual expression used to describe the full range between delirious joy and abject misery.

Origin: There is a simple musical explanation for the word. The original musical scale, devised by Guido d'Arezzo during the 11th century used letters of the Greek alphabet. The lowest note in the vocal scale was called 'gamma' (the third letter in the alphabet) and the highest note was called 'ut'. Therefore 'gamma' and 'ut' came together to describe the entire musical range. These days children use 'doh, ray, me' etc., to sing out the musical scale.

S

Saved by the bell

Meaning: Saved by a last minute intervention.

Origin: This is boxing slang that came into being in the latter half of the 19th century. A boxer who is in danger of losing a bout can be 'saved' from defeat by the bell that marks the end of a round.

Save your bacon

Meaning: To prevent a loss on a large scale, whether financially, professionally, or romantically—or it could perhaps even mean your life had been saved.

Origin: Bacon and other pig-related terms have been used as metaphors for people since as long ago. Pork was one of the few types of meat widely available and affordable throughout England, and for many it was the only meat they had to eat. This led to derision from both the aristocracy and the rich Norman lords, who, for example, would call Saxons 'hogs'. Writers and other artists have often used similar derogatory terms for country folk, such as 'swine' and 'pig' as well as 'hog'.

Scapegoat

Meaning: A person or group made to bear the blame for others or to suffer in their place.

Origin: Scapegoats are found in the Bible, Leviticus 16:8, 10, 26. The scapegoat was released, in a ceremony, into the wilderness to carry away the sins of Israel away from the camp. Nowadays, when we say we are a scapegoat, we say we are being blamed for somebody else's wrongdoing.

Scot free

Meaning: Without incurring payment; or escaping without punishment.

Origin: Dred Scott was a black slave born in Virginia, USA in 1799. In several celebrated court cases, right up to the USA Supreme Court in 1857, he attempted to gain his freedom. These cases all failed but Scott was later made a free man by his so-called owners, the Blow family. Knowing this, we might feel that we don't need to look further for the origin of 'scott free'.

Sent up the pole

Meaning: Being driven mad by something.

Origin: The actual pole in question is a ship's mast, in particular the part above the rigging. On the high seas this would be the most dangerous place to be.

Shaggy dog story

Meaning: Unconvincing origin; not necessarily to be believed.

Origin: The origin of this phrase is, in fact, a real shaggy dog story, dating from the 1800s. Apparently a wealthy gentleman, who owned a grand residence in Park Lane, lost his beloved shaggy dog during a walk across Hyde Park, opposite his home. The man was heartbroken and advertised extensively in The Times for the return of his valuable companion. Meanwhile, an American living in New York had heard the news and taken great pity on the dog's owner. He vowed he would search for a pet matching the description of the lost hound and deliver it to London on his next business visit, which he duly did. But when the New Yorker presented himself at the palatial London mansion, he was met by a poker-faced butler who, the story goes, looked down at the dog, bowed, winced and then exclaimed: 'But not as shaggy as that, sir!' The story provoked howls of laughter among London socialites, but was not entirely believed by everybody.

Shank's mare

Meaning: To use one's legs as a means of transport.

Origin: Shanks' (or shanks's) mare (or nag or pony) derives from the name of the lower part of the leg between the knee and ankle — the shank, nowadays more often known as the shin-bone or tibia. This was alluded to in the early form of this term — shank's nag.

Shell shocked

Meaning: When one is stunned and momentarily debilitated by something they have seen or heard.

Origin: During the First World War, soldiers experienced the introduction of heavy artillery and explosives such as had never been seen before in the field of conflict. It was during the trench warfare of 1915, after almost constant shelling from enemy guns, that a significant number of Allied casualties, suffering from what was described as shell shock, were reported. This was a relatively unheard-of disorder; it resulted in young men suffering from a wide range of both physical and psychological problems.

Shilly shallying

Meaning: One who is known to he undecided and hesitant about something or someone.

Origin: During the Middle Ages, a well-known phrase expressing uncertainty was 'shall I, shall I'. A variation on the theme is 'dilly dally' — a simple play on the word 'dally', meaning to linger or dawdle. The expression 'willy-nilly' indicates an action that will take place with or without the consent of the person on the receiving end.

Shiver my timbers

Meaning: Expression of anger or surprise; swear.

Origin: Used liberally by Robert Newton playing the role of a pirate in the film based on Robert Louis Stevenson's book *Treasure Island*.

Show your true colours

Meaning: To reveal one's true nature.

Origin: Warships used to fly multiple flags to confuse their enemies. However, the rules of warfare stated that a ship had to hoist its true flag before firing and hence, display its country's true colours.

Sick as a dog

Meaning: Someone being very sick.

Origin: The origin of the saying originates from the early 1700s where it was common to call something undesirable, dirty, or in this case, sick, to dogs. There are likely more literal explanations including the fact that diseases such as the plague would travel the globe via animals such as rats, birds, and even dogs. There was an epidemic illness spread by dogs and hence the saying was created.

A sight for sore eyes

Meaning: Finally a relief.

Origin: Jonathan Swift, author of *Gulliver's Travels*, first used this phrase in *A Complete Collection of Genteel and Ingenious Conversation*, 1738, with the line 'The Sight of you is good for sore Eyes.'

Sign the Pledge

Meaning: To give up drinking alcohol.

Origin: The source of this phrase can be traced to the height of the Temperance Movement during the 19th century which encouraged drinkers wishing to give up alcohol to 'sign the temperance pledge' and make a public declaration never to touch the evil stuff again.

Sirloin steak

Meaning: The favoured part of a loin of beef.

Origin: Folklore tells us that apparently the old tyrant enjoyed a feast in one of his castles to such an extent on one occasion that he actually bestowed a knighthood on a loin of beef he had dined on. And so, much to the great amusement of his court, the favoured cut became known thereafter as Sir Loin. The sirloin is, after all, the 'upper' cut of the loin of beef.

Skeleton in your closet

Meaning: A secret you try to keep hidden.

Origin: It first appeared in the 1800's. The reference to a 'skeleton' in this case was the danger from an infectious or hereditary disease. One theory is that prior to 1832, the extensive use of corpses for medical research was not allowed. The theory goes that in domestic houses in Elizabethan England, doctors would conceal in cupboards the illegally held skeletons they used for teaching.

Skin of your teeth

Meaning: To achieve something by the narrowest of margins.

Origin: This is a truly expressive phrase, which can be traced to the Bible, although it seems to have been misquoted somewhere along the way. The Book of Job (19:20): 'Job was with the skin of his teeth; everything else had been taken from him, including his possessions, health, family and friends.'

Sleep tight

Meaning: Sleep well.

Origin: During Shakespeare's time, mattresses were secured on bed frames by ropes. In order to make the bed firmer, one had to pull the ropes to tighten the mattress.

Smart aleck

Meaning: Someone just too clever for their own good.

Origin: It has been recorded that the most likely origin for this expression is the New York City con man and fraudster Aleck Hoag. During the 1840s, the scoundrel had his wife posing as a prostitute and between them they would rob their customers, knowing few men would report the crime to the police under such compromising circumstances. However, on some occasions the pair were caught, although Hoag managed to escape prosecution by bribing the officers involved. But then Hoag tried to be a little too clever by cutting the arresting policeman out of the deal, convinced this would be overlooked should previous police corruption become apparent during any prosecution but he was wrong and found himself in jail. Policemen in New York from then onwards used the expression 'smart aleck' to describe anybody pushing their luck too far.

Sneeze in public

Meaning: When we sneeze there is always somebody nearby, sometimes a complete stranger, who says 'Bless You', but why?

Origin: There was the medieval belief that sneezing expelled a person's soul from their living body, enabling an evil spirit or the devil to take possession instead. The only way for the 'clean' soul to return was to bless the person.

Someone just walked over my grave

Meaning: This is a remark often used when a person gets the shivers.

Origin: This expression came about thanks to an old wives' tale, which is a legend, fable or story that is invariably both ridiculous and amazing and only ever believed by the naïve or gullible. The 'wives' in this instance believed that an involuntary shiver is felt when the place where a person will eventually be buried is being walked upon, and this was seen as a reminder of that person's mortality.

In spades

Meaning: To a very high degree; in abundance.

Origin: The expression 'in spades', used to described a large amount, is a 20th century US word used in Bridge and card games, referring to spades as one of the highest ranking suits.

Speak of the devil

Meaning: A reference to someone who appears unexpectedly while being talked about.

Origin: This phrase is used to acknowledge the coincidence of someone arriving at a scene just at the time that they are being talked about. Clearly, nothing sinister is implied by this and it is just a jokey way of referring to the person's appearance. In fact, many people using the phrase might not be aware that, prior to the 20th century, the term wasn't meant lightheartedly at all. The full form goes like this—'speak of the Devil and he will appear'. The phrase originated in England, where it was, and still is, more often given as 'talk of the Devil'. The phrase is old and appears in various Latin and Old English texts from the 16th century. The Italian writer Giovanni Torriano has the first recorded version in contemporary English, in *Piazza Universale*, 1666: 'The English say, Talk of the Devil, and he's presently at your elbow.'

Spill the beans

Meaning: To reveal a secret.

Origin: In Ancient Greece, beans were used to vote for candidates entering various organizations. One container for each candidate was set out before the group members, who would place a white bean in the container if they approved of the candidate and a black bean if they did not. Sometimes a clumsy voter would accidentally knock over the jar, revealing all of the beans and allowing everyone to see the otherwise confidential votes.

Square meal

Meaning: A healthy, hearty dinner.

Origin: Nobody actually knows where this idiom came from, though the Royal Navy did serve meals on square plates at one point. 'Square' means to be honest and straightforward goes back to at least the 16th century, which is what the men who served the navy got—an honestly earned hearty meal.

Stay on the straight and narrow

Meaning: To stay out of trouble.

Origin: Biblical in origin. *Matthew 7:13/14* described the gates to heaven as 'strait' and the way to eternal life as 'narrow'.

Steal one's thunder

Meaning: To do something that takes attention away from what someone else has done.

Origin: The 18th century playwright John Dennis claimed to have invented a machine that could mimic the sound of thunder in the theatre. When rivals used the same trick, he complained they'd 'stolen his thunder'.

Stemming the flow of blood or water

Meaning: This is an idiom.

Origin: The expression can he traced back to the Viking invasions of the late eighth century and the old Nordic language they brought along with them. The Vikings used to build dams and the Norse word for one of those is *stemma*, which, loosely translated, means to 'dam up' or 'stop'.

Stick to your guns

Meaning: One who stands up for one's rights and beliefs no matter what happens.

Origin: This was a command given to sailors manning the guns on military boats. They were to stay at their posts even when the boat was being attacked by enemies. In the mid 1700s, the saying was also used for anyone who held onto their convictions whether we agreed with them or not.

In stitches

Meaning: Laughing uncontrollably.

Origin: Another Shakespearan coinage, although not used again until the 20th century. In *Twelfth Night*, 1602, Maria says: 'If you desire the spleen, and will laugh yourself into stitches, follow me.'

Streets are paved with gold

Meaning: This is an indication that a particular town or city is full of opportunity and well worth a visit.

Origin: George Colman the Younger wrote, in *The Heir-at-Law* (1797): 'Oh, London is a fine town, a very famous city, where all the streets are paved with gold, and all the maidens pretty.' This expression seemed to be coined in a popular legend that tells the story of Dick Whittington, who as a 13-year-old boy packed his worldly goods into his handkerchief, tied it on the end of a stick and made his way from Gloucestershire to London after hearing the pavements there were made of gold and silver.

Stuck up

Meaning: A person who is a little aloof and behaving in a superior manner.

Origin: The expression recalls the way peacocks habitually 'stick up' their tail feathers as if to display their importance or superiority over fellow peacocks.

Straight from the horse's mouth

Meaning: Getting information directly from a person or place is your most reliable source. The information is obtained first-hand, direct from the source or origin.

Origin: A horse's age can be easily determined by examining the size and shape of his teeth. Your information about the horse's age would be correct and, 'straight from the horse's mouth'.

Stump up a payment

Meaning: To make a payment or hand over money.

Origin: 'Stumpy' was the slang word for money during the 1800s, and 'to stumpy up' or 'stump up' was a regularly used phrase for paying rent or other bills that were due immediately.

Swan song

Meaning: A final gesture or performance, given before dying or retirement.

Origin: This term derived from the legend that, while they are mute during the rest of their lives, swans sing beautifully and mournfully just before they die. This isn't actually the case— swans, even the inaccurately named Mute Swans, have a variety of vocal sounds and they don't sing before they die.

T

Take the piss

Meaning: To ridicule someone.

Origin: One of the least desirable jobs was to collect human urine for the cloth-dying industry. Anyone in this line of work would be inclined to lie about what they did for a living. Anyone suspecting the truth might ask if he was, in actual fact, 'taking the piss'.

Taken to the cleaners

Meaning: A victim of a con. One who has been the victim of a con and, as a result, lost most or all of one's money.

Origin: During the 1800s, the expression 'to be cleaned out' was in regular use to explain a situation where a person had been 'stripped clean' or 'cleaned' of their possessions, either by fraud or as result of gambling. The phrase changed slightly during the 20th century with the introduction of dry cleaners.

Tanked up

Meaning: To get yourself to be rolling drunk on a Friday or Saturday night or, for that matter, at any time.

Origin: This phrase takes us back to the taverns and inns of medieval England when drinks were served in clay tankards. If a customer drank vast quantities of ale and then passed out, they were known as 'tankard'.

The abominable snowman

Meaning: This is a popular name given to a Yeti, the large man-like beast said to be living in the Himalayas.

Origin: A Tibetan legend described the Yeti as a fearsome creature with a near-human face that would raid remote mountain villages. The story was spread by the early European mountaineers attempting to conquer Mount Everest in the 1920s. By the 1950s, the legend was firmly established and enhanced by both Nicholas Blake's detective novel *The Case of the Abominable Snowman* and the film *The Abominable Snowman*, released in 1957. In the 1960s, the first man to reach the summit of Everest, Sir Edmund Hillary, claimed to have found large bear-like footprints when he was there in 1953, which only added to the legend. But why is it abominable? The answer can be found in the Tibetan word for Yeti, *Meetohkangmi* — *meetoh* meaning 'foul' and *kangmi* 'snowman'.

The backroom boys

Meaning: A group of people, male or female, who work away quietly, developing new ideas that would be of particular benefit to industry or commerce.

Origin: Scientists who are hard at work developing new products for a particular company might be nicknamed 'backroom boys'. In offices, administrators keep the whole business running smoothly with little or no thanks for their efforts, and they would also be known as backroom boys. The phrase was coined during the Second World War when Lord Beaverbrook, who was minister of aircraft production at the time, made a radio broadcast on 19 March 1941 during which he credited his research department for some inspiring inventions that helped to change the direction of the war.

The best thing since sliced bread

Meaning: The very best of something.

Origin: In 1912, Otto Frederick Rohwedder, of Iowa, USA, began work on a bread-slicing machine. The machine took time to perfect, mainly due to the difficulty in keeping sliced bread fresh, but in 1927 a waxed paper bag solved that problem for him. The first slicing machine was installed the following year at the Chillicothe Baking Company, owned by a friend of Otto's called M. Frank Bench, and on 7 July 1928, the first sliced loaf was sold. Known as the Sliced Kleen Maid Bread, the product was an instant success and customers were delighted with the neat and even slices, which were so easy to use. Thus Otto became known as the father of sliced bread.

The bitter end

Meaning: To the limit of one's efforts — to the last extremity.

Origin: Bitter has been an adjective meaning acrid or sour tasting since the year 725 AD at least. The word was in common use in the Middle Ages and Shakespeare uses it numerous times in his plays and poems, as do many other dramatists.

The kiss of death

Meaning: Heralds the demise of something.

Origin: Its roots rest in the Italian mafia, where someone who's been marked for death receives the metaphorical kiss prior to execution.

The third degree

Meaning: Long or arduous interrogations.

Origin: The phrase relates to the various degrees of murder in the criminal code. It may also be credited to Thomas F. Byrnes, a 19th-century New York City policeman who used the pun 'Third Degree Byrnes' when describing his hardnosed questioning style. It is most likely derived from the Freemasons, a centuries-old fraternal organization whose members undergo rigorous questioning and examinations before becoming 'third degree' members, or 'master masons'.

The upper crust

Meaning: High society, social or financial elite.

Origin: Until the 19th century, bread was baked in stone ovens. The loaves would be sliced horizontally. The lower crust was inedible because it had been in contact with the oven floor and was too hard and dirty to eat and used as a plate or given to the servants to eat. The upper crust was baked just right and was clean and given to the lord and lady of the castle.

The whole kit and caboodle

Meaning: Absolutely everything; the whole lot.

Origin: The word 'caboodle' comes from the Dutch word *boedel*, which means 'possessions', while kit has been a short word used for 'equipment' for centuries. Collectively the 'whole kit and caboodle' and has meant 'everything you have in your possession'.

The world is your oyster

Meaning: Anything is possible and hard work and careful decisions will lead to great success in the future.

Origin: It comes, like so many other phrases, from Shakespeare. In his play *The Merry Wives of Windsor* (1597), there is an exchange between Falstaff and Pistol in Act 2, Scene ii:
'FALSTAFF: I will not lend thee a penny.
PISTOL: Why then, the world is mine oyster, which I with sword shall open.'

Thinking cap

Meaning: To take time to consider a problem and hopefully solve it.

Origin: In the very early law courts, it became traditional for a judge to wear a black cap to show the court he had heard all the evidence he needed in order to reach a decision. It was a signal that he was now in the process of considering his verdict and would soon be passing sentence. In later years, this practice was restricted to the passing of a death sentence only, but in either case this was the original 'thinking cap'.

Three sheets to the wind

Meaning: Being totally drunk.

Origin: Sailors had a lot of terms for being drunk and they all related to the ship. Being tipsy was 'a sheet in the wind's eye' and being hammered was a full 'three sheets to the wind'. The sheets in question were actually the ropes that held down the sails, so if all three ropes were loose, the sails would billow about like a drunken sailor.

Throw in the towel

Meaning: To admit defeat and give up on an idea completely.

Origin: The expression was originally 'to throw in the sponge' and reflects the common practice during boxing matches, and bare-knuckle fighting, of a contestant's seconds accepting a defeat for their man by throwing in the sponge or towel, during a round, as a signal for the referee to stop the bout. It is an admission of defeat.

Through thick and thin

Meaning: To go through all forms of obstacles that are put in one's way.

Origin: 'Through thick and thin' is one of the English language's older expressions and one that has maintained its figurative meaning over many centuries. It is venerable enough to date from the times when England was still a predominantly wooded country, with few roads and where animals grazed on what was known as wood pasture, that is, mixed woodland and grass. The phrase originated as 'through thicket and thin wood', which was a straightforward literal description of any determined progress through the 'thick' English countryside.

Tittle tattle

Meaning: Any minor piece of gossip or news.

Origin: Tattle is an Old English word for 'idle chat' or 'chatter', therefore to add the 'tittle' in front of 'tattle' reinforced the idea of very small talk.

Toady

Meaning: A sycophant, a person who will do anything to earn a superior's respect and affection.

Origin: During the Middle Ages, quack doctors, or charlatans, would employ an impoverished person (usually a starving man who would do absolutely anything to earn a crust) to work with them while they tried to sell their remedies. Typically, the unfortunate person would consume an apparently poisonous toad, in front of a gathering, so that the doctor could then prove his remedies would cure the contaminated man. Naturally, the toad was not poisonous in the first place. If it had been, then the man would have died as the quack's remedies never worked anyway, but the doctor's 'toady' was still prepared to eat in public a live creature, and a disgusting one at that, for the sake of a loaf of bread.

To be blackballed

Meaning: To be excluded from a club or society by other members who vote against an application for membership or being left out of any social event or gathering.

Origin: The phrase became known in 1770 when the practice of 'balling' was adopted by the London gentlemen's clubs. The idea was that if a new member was proposed, then every existing member of the club would be asked if he had any objection to the new addition. Members were asked to place a white or black ball anonymously into a symbolic urn or bag. One single black ball was enough to refuse a membership and nobody at the club would ever know who had opposed the application.

To be grinning like a Cheshire cat

Meaning: To be very pleased with yourself and constantly smiling, perhaps somewhat foolishly.

Origin: The mysterious Cheshire Cat appeared and then disappeared in Lewis Carroll's *Alice's Adventures in Wonderland* (1865). In the story, the Cheshire Cat gradually fades away until only his grin remains. The book became so popular all over the world that many regard this as the source of the expression. However, the phrase, and the related one, cheesy grin, has long been in use and is thought to relate to the face of a grinning cat stamped on all cheeses produced in Cheshire since the 12th century.

Toe the line

Meaning: To conform to an established standard or political program.

Origin: There is some confusion between 'toe the line' and the frequently seen misspelling 'tow the line'. The 'tow' version is no doubt encouraged by the fact that ropes or cables on ships are often called lines and that 'tow lines' are commonplace nautical items. The earlier meaning of 'to toe the line' was to position one's toes next to a marked line in order to be ready to start a race, or some other undertaking. In the 19th century, we wouldn't have been limited to lines when it came to placing our feet, but would have had a choice of what to toe—a mark, scratch, crack or trig (a line or small trench).

To be having kittens

Meaning: A hysterically nervous person, who is petrified about a forthcoming event.

Origin: During the Middle Ages doctors apparently believed that if a pregnant woman was experiencing pains then she must be 'bewitched' and had a litter of kittens inside her womb that were clawing at her. Witches, it was said, could provide the potions that would destroy the imagined kittens. Incredibly, as late as the 17th century the legal term for 'obtaining an abortion' was still presented in the law courts as 'removing cats in the belly'.

To be made of sterner stuff

Meaning: To be strong both mentally and emotionally, having firm resolve and not buckling easily under pressure.

Origin: This is from the inventive prose of William Shakespeare. In his play *Julius Caesar* (1599), Mark Antony, when speaking at Caesar's funeral, responds to the claim that he is ruthless and determined: 'Did this in Caesar seem- ambitious? When that the poor have cried, Caesar hath wept; Ambition should be made of sterner stuff.'

To be on the side of the angels

Meaning: To be in agreement with those who are perceived to be beyond reproach, the so-called ruling classes and the morally sound. In other words, they think you are always right.

Origin: This is a phrase that can be traced directly to a speech given by Queen Victoria's favorite politician and a former prime minister, Benjamin Disraeli.

To be whiter than white

Meaning: A person who is seen as pure, innocent and virtuous, never implicated in any wrongdoing.

Origin: The phrase has been in use since the end of the 16th century, being lifted directly from Shakespeare's poem *Venus and Adonis* (1593), which includes the line: 'Teaching the sheets a whiter hew than white'.

To bell the cat

Meaning: Any dangerous task carried out at great personal risk.

Origin: The origin of this phrase and why we use it can be found in William Langland's *Piers Plowman* (1377). This contains the tale of a family of mice who were constantly being terrorized by the fat, grumpy cat of the neighborhood. One day the mouse household held a family meeting to discuss how they could best deal with the surprise attacks and the youngest mouse came up with the notion of tying a bell around the cat's neck, so that all the mice would be able to hear him coming. This idea delighted all the others and they danced around in celebration until the wisest old mouse said, 'That's all very well, but who will actually bell the cat?' (No one did in the end.)

To blow a raspberry

Meaning: A show of contempt by making a rude noise.

Origin: There are many that are more easily explained, such as 'blowing a kiss', 'blow away the cobwebs', 'blowing your brains out', 'blowing your mind', 'blowing over', 'blowing your socks off'', 'blow your top', 'blow me tight' and 'blowing my horn'.

To box and cox

Meaning: To alternate between two situations simultaneously, usually in a half-hearted manner and often with disastrous consequences.

Origin: *Box and Cox — A Romance of Real Life in One Act* is the title of a play by John Maddison Morton in 1847. The story tells of John Box and James Cox, two men who were renting the very same room from an unscrupulous landlady, Mrs Bouncer. One of the men worked all day long and the other all night, so were quite unaware of the presence of each other in the room, although they did meet twice a day on the stairs. Eventually the deception is revealed and, in a farcical scene, the two men then play dice for the room. The whole episode ends happily with the discovery that they are, in fact, long-lost brothers.

To broach a subject

Meaning: To start a conversation in a general way with one or more people.

Origin: The root of this term can be tracked down to the alehouses and hotels of London several centuries ago. In order to gain access to and draw ale from a new barrel, a barman would hammer a peg, known as a 'broach', into a hole at the base of the barrel. This was known as 'broaching the barrel' which started the beer flowing so the fun could begin.

To camp it up

Meaning: To perform in an effeminate and flamboyant manner in an attempt to draw attention to oneself.

Origin: This phrase became applied to overt homosexuality. It is recorded that trails or groups of civilians would follow a marching army, providing various services such as sales of alcohol, washer women or male and female prostitutes. As they would also camp nearby, this could perhaps be where the associated expression camp as a row of tents, derives from.

Toffee nosed

Meaning: Snobbish; supercilious; stuck-up.

Origin: The origin of 'toffee-nosed' has nothing to do with the sugary, brown sweet, but derives from 'toff', which was the slang term given by the lower-classes in Victorian England to stylishly-dressed upper-class gentlemen.

To double cross

Meaning: To cheat somebody, or to betray a confidence.

Origin: This expression began life in the Middle Ages when Venetian merchants would affect allegiance to fellow Westerners by making the sign of the cross in the way Westerners did, and then show the same loyalty to Easterners by crossing themselves in the way Easterners used to. This divided loyalty led to the introduction of the term 'double crosser'.

To eat crow

Meaning: Personal discomfort, humiliation and embarrassment.

Origin: Similar to the English idiom 'eating humble pie', the phrase has its root in the folklore of the late 19th century and a story that was apparently reported in the Atlanta Constitution in 1888. According to the story, during an armistice of the Anglo-American War (1812–14), a New Englander made the mistake of crossing the English lines, while out hunting, and shot dead a crow. An unarmed English officer heard of this and resolved to punish the offender. He found the American and praised him for his marksmanship, gaining his confidence enough to be given the weapon for a trial shot himself. At this point, the officer advised the American he was trespassing and turned the gun on him, forcing him to take a bite out of the dead crow, which the trembling American duly did. When the officer was satisfied the American was suitably humiliated, he gave back the weapon and told him to return to his own lines. At which point, the American turned the tables and forced the hapless Brit to eat the remainder of the crow.

To get your kit off

Meaning: To undress completely.

Origin: This is of recent origin and applied to removing military kit, although in the early 1990s British journalists began to apply it to actresses, actors and anyone else stripping naked.

To give someone the willies

Meaning: To arouse unease and fear in them.

Origin: In bygone days a willow tree was called a 'willy'. The weeping 'willy' tree (called 'weeping' because of its long trailing branches resembling streams of tears) has long been associated with grief and mourning.

To give the thumbs up

Meaning: A sign of approval, often given as a gesture, while thumbs down indicates disapproval.

Origin: Both gestures are used throughout the world, regardless of language or culture, and their origin can be found in the Roman amphitheatres of two thousand years ago. If a gladiator found himself at the mercy of his opponent, he would look to the emperor for a thumbs-up gesture to show approval for his fighting skills. If the crowd were shouting '*mitte, mitte*', meaning 'let him go free', then a thumbs-up gesture would follow and he would be spared. At the very least he would hope to see a closed-hand gesture (*poilicem cornprimere*) as an indication that he had fought well, but the thumbs in a downward position and the chant of '*lugula*' meant a horrible end for the person in front of thousands of Romans baying for his blood.

To give a barnstorming performance

Meaning: To execute something in a particularly exhilarating fashion—such as a public speaker delivering a rousing speech, or an actor or musician thrilling an audience.

Origin: The original barnstormers were just second-rate thespians who toured the American countryside in the early 19th century, performing to locals in a barn. These actors were famous for their exaggerated style, often producing rousing theatre (akin to the fury of a storm) in order to compensate for their lack of dramatic skill. The expression passed over into wider use thanks to the US politicians of the time who hijacked the actors' style and toured the states giving stirring, excitable speeches, typically also in barns, in an effort to win votes.

To ham it up

Meaning: An amateur or unskilled thespian, a jobbing actor who remains largely unknown and only ever has the bit parts in a play.

Origin: This reference first appeared in print in 1882 and was directed at the travelling black and white minstrel shows in America. The famous entertainers used to perform a ballad called 'The Ham-Fat Man' which is said to refer to low-paid actors who used ham fat to remove their stage make-up after a show. Apparently the phrase was later shortened to 'ham' and directed at any substandard performer. Hence boxers who display little dexterity are known as ham-fisted, an expression extended to fumbling attempts at just about anything. Also, amateur radio enthusiasts who enjoy tuning in and broadcasting goodness knows what to each other, are still called radio hams.

To have more than you can shake a stick at

Meaning: To have far more of anything than you really need.

Origin: This expression is said to have a farming origin, in particular sheep farming. If a shepherd had more sheep than he could control with his crook (stick) then it is easy to see how the term came to be applied. There is another American origin of a military kind. After George Washington was once seen waving a ceremonial wooden sword over the British troops he had recently defeated, other American generals began to use the expression to justify themselves when they had not been quite as successful as the great man himself was in battle. 'We had more men to fight than you could wave a stick at' was apparently a common excuse for failure on the battlefield.

To have bought the farm

Meaning: This is a well-known American expression meaning 'to have died'.

Origin: There are several suggested origins, one being a sentimental line in a US war film, which has a character from the Mid-West yearning for home and telling friends that when the war is over he plans to return to the country, buy a farm and settle down. When the character is later killed in action, his buddy sentimentally remarks: 'Well, I guess Joe has bought his farm now.' The second suggested, and more likely, origin leads us to the early days of aviation when the great pioneers were invariably rich playboys, such as Gordon Bennett, who were living life on the edge of danger. If and when aircraft crashed into farms or remote farmland, the estate of the deceased pilot would be held responsible for any damage and was invariably forced to pay substantial costs. Such payments would usually be enough for the farmer to redeem a mortgage or to buy a farm outright. Dead aviators were thus often known to have paid for or 'bought the farm'. Also the phrase has a religious origin, on the basis that the Old Testament refers to heaven as 'a farm for the soul'. A person killed, especially in the service of the good Lord, had a place in heaven, hence 'bought the farm'.

To have a hunch

Meaning: To have an instinctive feeling about an outcome.

Origin: This expression is American in origin, dating from the early 1900s. It derives from a gambling superstition that suggested rubbing the hump of a hunchback would bring good fortune. This in turn connects to a medieval belief that hunchbacks were possessed and empowered by the devil to see into the future.

To hit the ground running

Meaning: A person or event getting off to a successful start, straight into action.

Origin: Originally it was an American phrase, which can be traced directly to the military training schools of both the First and Second World Wars. Foot soldiers, paratroopers and marines were all trained extensively to jump and land on their feet, either from boats, aircraft or jeeps, so they could get on with the business at hand without delay. 'Hit the ground running' was a frequently heard shout from the training officer on manoeuvres and the expression had become widespread by the end of the Second World War. It had passed into regular usage by the time of the business boom during the 1980s when rapid success was a defining feature of the decade.

To know where all the bodies are buried

Meaning: Persons in a very strong position with their employers as it means they know all the inner secrets of an organization, and this may be damaging if that person should ever leave to join a rival company.

Origin: It derives from the cult American movie *Citizen Kane* (1941). In one famous scene, Susan Alexander, Kane's estranged wife, remarks of the butler at Xanadu: 'but he knows where all the bodies are buried'. The phrase immediately caught on and has been particularly popular on both sides of the Atlantic since the cut-throat business boom of the 1980s.

To laugh like a drain

Meaning: To laugh out loud in an uncontrollable manner.

Origin: The phrase is British in origin, dating to just after the Second World War, and reflects the echoing gurgle often heard emanating from the sewers and drains beneath the City of London.

To lead someone up the garden path

Meaning: To mislead a person completely.

Origin: The place where a seduction could be carried out, in those stiff Victorian days, after the promise of marriage.

To lionize someone

Meaning: To treat someone as a celebrity and to show them off in front of others.

Origin: From 1834, all exotic animals gifted to the King of England would be kept and displayed at the Tower of London. Such creatures from far-off continents included leopards, bears, wolves, lynxes and the star attraction, the African lions. The great and the good of London society and royal circles would often entertain important guests at the Tower, and any celebrities might find themselves the center of attention during such gatherings and sometimes put on display by their hosts—'shown off', just like the lions.

To make no bones

Meaning: To speak plainly without minding about causing offence; coming straight to the point, in other words.

Origin: The origin of the expression can be found in the game of dice, which was once called 'bones' after the material they were carved from. Similarly, in Old French there was an expression that may be translated as 'sliding of dice' that was used to describe the act of softening something that has been said. Another expression, 'you can pick the bones out of that' suggests a piece of work is so good no errors will be found anywhere, just as you would find no bones in a perfect piece of meat or in a stew.

To do a moonlight flit

Meaning: To take leave without notice or permission and to move on to another place.

Origin: The word flit is an Old English and Scottish word, meaning to move house. Between then and the 1930s, it was common for people to disappear quickly from their lodgings under cover of darkness, leaving bills unpaid and using only the moonlight to find their way to a new town and place to live.

To muff something

Meaning: To make an easy mistake or, in the context of sport, to fail to catch a ball. Also the person involved, who is perceived as awkward, clumsy and dull.

Origin: It has been in use for centuries and possibly originates from a play called *The Rival Candidates* (1774) in which the character Mr Harry Muff appears as a clumsy, blundering old fool. 'Muff' became more widely recognized and used, particularly by schoolboys.

To present something warts and all

Meaning: To make no attempt to cover any defects or hide unsightly detail.

Origin: It has always been customary for portrait painters to soften the features of their subjects by removing blemishes and facial lines from their work to improve upon nature. But when Oliver Cromwell, as Lord Protector of England in the mid-17th century, commissioned Sir Peter Lely to paint his portrait, he issued the artist with the following instructions: 'I desire you would use all your skill to paint my picture truly like I am and not flatter me at all. Remark all these roughness, pimples, warts and everything as you see me, otherwise I will never pay you a farthing for it.' The end result does indeed include a large wart just below Cromwell's lower lip.

To push the envelope

Meaning: To attempt to extend the current limits of performance. To innovate, or go beyond commonly accepted boundaries.

Origin: This phrase came into general use following the publication of Tom Wolfe's book about the space program, *The Right Stuff*, 1979. The envelope here isn't the container for letters, but the mathematical envelope, which is defined as 'the locus of the ultimate intersections of consecutive curves'. In a two-dimensional example, the set of lines described by the various positions of a ladder sliding down a wall forms an envelope—in this case an arc, gently curving away from the intersection of the wall and floor. Inside that envelope you will be hit by the ladder; outside you won't.

To put a spoke in someone's wheel

Meaning: To deliberately disrupt others' plans and restrict progress.

Origin: Horse-drawn carts all had wheels made out of solid, circular, wooden discs. Holes were bored through the front wheels into which a pole or a peg, known as the 'spoke', could be placed, like a form of brake, in order to either restrict the speed of the wheel (when going downhill) or stop the cart altogether. The word 'spoke' was first recorded in the early 1600s and derives from the Dutch word *speek*, which became spike in Old English and later developed into the word 'spoke'.

To steal a march

Meaning: A person who gains an advantage by taking action before they either realize what is happening or are ready for it.

Origin: This is a military expression and dates to around 1770, revealing the tactic of an army marching through the night, while their enemy slept, in order to occupy a strategic position, ready to fight, before the enemy had even woken up and thought what to have for breakfast.

To a T

Meaning: Exactly; properly; precisely.

Origin: The expression 'to a T', is often extended to form other phrases: 'down to a T', 'suits to a T', 'fits to a T', 'generous to a T', etc. It is also found in advertising copy like 'Golf to a tee' and 'coffee to a tea'. The correct spellings are many: 'T', 'tee' or 'tea'. 'Tea' is the easiest to deal with as it appears in no early citations of the expression and is clearly just a misspelling. The proposed derivations that assume the phrase is 'to a tee' are as follows: The phrase derives from the sports of golf or curling, which have a tee as the starting or ending point respectively. The curling usage would seem to match the meaning better as the tee is the precise center of the circle in which players aim to stop their stones. 'T-shirt' is a name of American origin referring to the shape of the garment in question. 'T-shirts' are a 20th century invention. 'T-square' has something going for it, in that a T-square is a precise drawing instrument, but also lacks any other evidence to link it to the phrase.

To tighten your belt

Meaning: Make a sacrifice to keep above board, a temporary solution to a short-term economic problem.

Origin: In the Depression era there was little money for anything including food so people had to be very careful with what they had to make two ends meet.

To trim your sails

Meaning: To reduce your spending, and other activities, in line with your present circumstances.

Origin: In heavy weather, sailors will reef the sails when the wind is strong and let them out again in calmer waters. Same as 'cut your coat according to your cloth'.

Touch wood

Meaning: The traditional way to ensure a favourable outcome once we have mentioned it is to find a nearby piece of wood and touch it.

Origin: Many believe the tradition is Christian in origin and that the wood in question is that of a crucifix or a rosary. Others think it found its origin from the children's game of tag, and a participant is only safe when touching wood. There was also a children's game known as 'touch-iron'. Also the ancient beliefs of the Druids, who inhabited England before the Romans, that all the good and protective spirits in the world lived inside trees.

To sow your wild oats

Meaning: The pursuit of wild, possibly illegal and undoubtedly immoral practices while in the full bloom of youth.

Origin: The expression has been in use for over four centuries, deriving from the notion that impulsive young men would scatter only wild and uncultured seed here, there and everywhere, while older men, being wiser and more experienced, would take care to sow their cultivated seed only on fertile ground. Wild oats (or wild seed) produce weeds! Now it refers to indulgence in regular sexual activity for either sex. But when we consider the actual meaning of the expression—'to be getting your share of seed'—it rather loses its youthful, romantic sense, especially when applied to the fairer sex.

To send somebody up the river

Meaning: To imprison.

Origin: New York's Sing Sing Jail lies up the Hudson River from New York City and convicts were sent by boat to be incarcerated there. Since 1891, the phrase has been used in the States in respect to jailing a person.

To turn the tables

Meaning: To reverse the situation or conditions completely.

Origin: This expression derives from the old practice, during board games such as draughts or chess, of actually turning the board around once you were in a dominant position, to see if you could still beat an opponent from the disadvantaged position they themselves had been in.

To take the cake

Meaning: To be outrageous enough to deserve merit.

Origin: There was a game whereby couples would parade arm in arm around a barn and were judged by the others on the style and grace of their walk. The winning couple would be given a cake as a prize and the most flamboyant and entertaining of them could expect to hear cries of 'they take the cake'. This pastime was known as the cakewalk, which is also a well-known expression for something that is easy to achieve.

Turn a blind eye

Meaning: A situation when we know what is going on and what is about to happen, but fail to take any action to alter the situation.

Origin: It is a phrase emanating from one of the most significant events in British naval history. During the Battle of Copenhagen, in 1801, the commander of the British fleet, Admiral Sir Hyde Parker, watched as Horatio Nelson launched an attack on the Danish navy. At one point, Parker felt that the fleet was taking unnecessary risks and bearing unacceptable losses, so he ordered Nelson, via a series of flags, to disengage with the enemy. But when Nelson's officers pointed out the order, he famously raised a telescope to his blind eye and replied: 'Order, what order? I see no ships.' Nelson then returned his attention to the battle and soundly defeated the Danes. On his return to London, he was made a viscount and put in overall command of the Channel fleet, which led to his defining moment at the Battle of Trafalgar in 1805.

U

Under your wing

Meaning: To take a person under your wings is to provide them with friendly encouragement, advice and protection.

Origin: The source can be traced to the Bible. In *Matthew 23:37*, Jesus expresses his sorrow at what has become of Jerusalem and declares his wish to protect his people, like a hen will protect her chicks by spreading her wings so that they can find safety and shelter beneath them.

Upset the apple cart

Meaning: Throw plans and intentions into confusion.

Origin: During the 8th century, the 'apple cart' was a wrestling term for the upper body, and to 'upset the apple cart' meant to throw an opponent to the ground and scupper his chances of winning.

Up to the mark

Meaning: To be acceptable.

Origin: The 'mark' is seen as a recognized standard, and that is exactly what it was initially. Since 1697, when the Britannia standard was introduced, all gold and silver had been stamped with a 'hallmark' to prove its authenticity.

Up to scratch

Meaning: Acceptable.

Origin: It's a boxing term. At one time a line was scratched on the ground to mark the point where the fighters would meet. By failing to come up to the scratch, one would default the match.

Use your loaf

Meaning: To show common sense and intelligence.

Origin: This derives from the simple 'use your loaf of bread', meaning head in cockney rhyming slang. There is a second suggestion for the origin of this phrase, one that can be found in the archives of the American Civil War. The story tells us that Confederate soldiers would receive a freshly baked loaf of bread each day as part of their ration. When engaging Federal positions, soldiers were known to spear their loaf with a bayonet, place a hat upon it and hold it up from their covered position to see if the bobbing head attracted any gunfire. This practice was apparently known as using your loaf.

V

Vandalism

Meaning: Mindless idiots who enjoy breaking up and damaging anything they see, all in the name of fun.

Origin: The original useless, mindless idiots were a Teutonic race. In northeastern Germany throughout the fifth and sixth centuries they were known as the Vandals. The original use of the word 'vandalism' was to describe the wilful and unnecessary destruction of works of art.

Veg out

Meaning: Relax in a slothful and mindless manner.

Origin: This phrase is from the association of vegetables with mental incapacity; in the way that mentally disabled people are sometimes referred to as vegetables.

Vice-versa

Meaning: The reverse of the previous statement.

Origin: The English language has many expressions that refer to things being the wrong way around—'inside out', 'upside down', 'topsy-turvy' and 'the cart before the horse'.

W

Walk the plank

Meaning: A death sentence where the sentenced was made to walk with his hands tied behind his back, blindfolded, off a plank of wood into the sea.

Origin: Though there is no basis for the incident but a seaman George Wood had confessed that he and his shipmates had made some others to forcibly 'walk the plank' in the face of danger.

Waking up on the wrong side of the bed

Meaning: Waking up in a bad mood.

Origin: The left side of the body or anything having to do with the left was often associated with being considered sinister. To ward off evil, innkeepers made sure the left side of the bed was pushed against a wall, so guests had no other option but to get up on the right side of the bed.

Washing their hands of something

Meaning: Declaring that they no longer wish to be involved in the matter and will therefore not be implicated in the outcome of events.

Origin: The suggestion is that things are bound to go wrong and dissociation is the best course of action. The origin of the phrase can be found in the Bible. In the passage describing the trial of Jesus (*Matthew* 27:24), Pontius Pilate, who was in charge of sentencing him, declares to the masses that Jesus is innocent as far as he could tell but the crowd bay for blood and demand an execution. When Pilate realizes his appeal is accomplishing nothing, apart from inciting the people to riot, he takes a bowl of water and announces: 'I am innocent of the blood of this righteous man. You see to it.'

Wearing your heart on your sleeve

Meaning: Someone who is prepared to show their affection openly and obviously.

Origin: During the Middle Ages, and the great tournaments where noble knights battled for honour and prestige, it was common for a lady to 'give her heart' to a knight at such occasions in the form of a handkerchief or other token of affection. The knight would then enter the lists with the lady's 'heart' pinned to his sleeve, for all the spectators to see.

Whistle-blower

Meaning: A person who tries to raise the alarm about a problem and publicizes it inside and/or outside of his/her organization.

Origin: 'Whistle-blowers' are people who attempt to draw their superiors' attention to something they believe to be wrong and, if they fail in that attempt and if they feel strongly enough about the matter, go public. The expression 'whistle blower' was used literally well before it gained its current figurative meaning. Lots of people blew whistles; hunters were said to 'whistle down the wind' when they let their falcons loose to fly. Sailors, when needing a wind to free a becalmed ship, would 'whistle for it'. The first profession to be labeled as the 'whistle blowers' was the US police, who blew whistles to attract attention to wrongdoing. More recently, football referees have also been called 'whistle blowers'. The new use of the expression began in the 1960s and the earliest examples of its use are found in journalistic reports of the My Lai massacre in the Vietnam War, in which several hundred civilians were murdered. In the 19th century we had 'whistle blowers', in the 20th we had 'whistle-blowers' and now we have 'whistleblowers'. This changing of an expression into a word, with the intervening hyphenated phase, is one of the most common ways we form new words. There are many examples, from Shakespeare's coinages 'birthplace', 'bloodstained' and 'barefaced'.

Wide berth

Meaning: To avoid someone with a distance

Origin: At sea a berth is the place in which a ship drops anchor, and berths are allocated to all boats in a harbour. But any boat, large or small, will float around on the tide in any direction, to the limit of its anchor rope. Therefore when anchoring your vessel for the night, it would be wise to give the other boats in the harbour a wide berth lest they move on the tide and collide with yours.

Willy-nilly

Meaning: 'Whether it is with or against your will' and also 'in an unplanned, haphazard fashion'. We tend to use the latter of these meanings today; the former was the accepted meaning when the term was first coined.

Origin: The early meaning of the word, *nill* is key to this. In early English *nill* was the opposite of will a contraction of 'ne will'. That is, *will* meant to want to do something, *nill* meant to want to avoid it. So, combining the willy—'I am willing' and nilly—'I am unwilling' expresses the idea that it doesn't matter to me one way or the other. The Latin phrase *'nolens, volens'* means the same thing, although it isn't clear whether the English version is a simple translation of that.

Winning the plaudits

Meaning: One who gets acclaim or approval of those whom you seek to impress.

Origin: The root of the expression is Latin is from the word *plaudite* ('applaud') that was traditionally shouted out by Roman actors at the end of each performance to indicate to the audience the show had ended.

With bells on

Meaning: Enthusiastically, eagerly.

Origin: The first record of this phrase in print is in F. Scott Fitzgerald's *The Beautiful and the Damned*, 1922: 'All-ll-ll righty. I'll be there with bells!'

White elephant

Meaning: Any possession that is burdensome, useless, unwanted or cost a lot to keep, becoming more trouble than it is worth.

Origin: The legend in ancient Siam, now Thailand, a king gave a white elephant to someone whom he did not like. The albino elephant was considered sacred and holy in ancient times. Keeping a white elephant was a very expensive undertaking, since the owner had to provide the elephant with special food and provide access for people who wanted to worship it. The recipient could not get rid of the elephant because it was a gift from the King. The gift would, in most cases, ruin the recipient. In the nineteenth century the phrase was used at church bazaars called 'white elephant sales' where donors could bring unwanted items.

Working up to the collar

Meaning: Putting in real effort to get a job done.

Origin: The 'collar' referred to here is one worn by a horse or ox when pulling a heavy cart or perhaps a plough. Animals who worked with the collar straining tightly around their shoulders were obviously pulling heavy loads and therefore working extremely hard, while those with the collar set more loosely around their necks were clearly not having to drag such heavy weights and therefore not working to their full capacity. It is a farming expression that has been part of the English language for centuries.

Worth one's salt

Meaning: To be effective and efficient; deserving of one's pay.

Origin: Sodium chloride, a.k.a. salt, is essential for human life and, until the invention of canning and refrigeration, was the primary method of preservation of food. Not surprisingly, it has long been considered valuable. To be 'worth one's salt' is to be worth one's pay. Our word salary derives from the Latin salarium, (sal is the Latin word for salt). There is some debate over the origin of the word salarium, but most scholars accept that it was the money allowed to Roman soldiers for the purchase of salt. Roman soldiers weren't actually paid in salt, as some suggest. They were obliged to buy their own food, weapons etc. and had the cost of these deducted from their wages in advance.

Writing on the wall

Meaning: A particular, negative event that is inevitable and virtually unavoidable.

Origin: The Book of Daniel in the Bible tells the story of King Belshazzar who was feasting in Babylon while boasting about the power of his idols. God, on hearing this, diverted the River Euphrates so that Belshazzar's enemies could breach the walls of the city. As the king raised God's goblet high above his head, a hand appeared and wrote the words *'Mene, Mene, Tekel, Parsin'* which translates as 'Numbered, Numbered, Weighed, Divided'.

This was meant as a warning to the king of what was about to happen, but Belshazzar was uncertain of the meaning so he called upon Daniel to explain it to him. Daniel told Belshazzar that God had numbered the days left to him as king and that his reign was about to end. It was a warning the Persians were about to invade and take over. For the king, the writing was truly on the wall.

Wrong side of the tracks

Meaning: To live on the less socially desirable part of town.

Origin: In the 1800s, train tracks often divided a town into rich and poor sections. The rich people lived on the side of the track where the smoke from the trains didn't blow and the poor lived on the wrong side of the tracks where the smoke did, and was considered the dangerous side.

X

Xanthic

Meaning: Yellow or yellowish.

Origin: French *xanthique.*

X marks

Meaning: The exact location.

Origin: Originally an explanatory caption to a newspaper photograph or drawing of 'the scene of crime' in which a cross showed the position of the victim's body.

Xiphoid

Meaning: Shaped like a sword; *ensiform.*

Origin: Classical Greek *xiphoeides*, 'sword-shaped'; from *xiphos*, 'sword' + *eides*, '-oid'.

Y

Yada, yada

Meaning: A way to notify a person that what they're saying is predictable or boring.

Origin: This phrase has many alternate forms, which include 'yatata yatata', 'yadda yadda', and 'yada yada.' There's also the phrase 'blah blah blah' that essentially shares the same meaning. The saying, with its current 'and so on and so forth' meaning, looks to have appeared somewhere in the mid 1900s in its 'yatata yatata' form, as shown in the Tucson Daily Citizen from 1947, where it reads:

'What I purely love are those letters which say: 'Buster, you are just putting words in my trap, and furthermore, yatata yataya...' Because that way you know you are apt to keep eating if you can stir up even a small portion of the people.'

Yankee

Meaning: A Yank is US and European slang for an American.

Origin: Originally the Native American Indians used the words *yengees, yanghis* and *yankees* to describe English and French settlers. Dutch settlers who arrived at the turn of the 18th century immediately began to use the word to describe all Americans.

Yellow belly

Meaning: A coward.

Origin: The term 'yellow-belly' is an archetypal American term, but began life in England in the late 18th century as a mildly derogatory nickname.

You can't judge a book by its cover

Meaning: One should not form an opinion on someone or something based purely on what is seen on the surface, because after taking a deeper look, the person or thing may be very different than what was expected.

Origin: If someone is looking for a book to buy and read, the first thing that will probably grab their attention is the cover of the book. Based solely on the cover, a person may decide whether a book is or is not for them. As a result, they may overlook a book simply because the cover appears plain or uninteresting to them. However, if the person would have opened up the book and looked at what's inside instead of overlooking it, they may have found it to be pretty interesting after all. This expression is also applied to people. People are often judged solely based upon their outward appearance. If one were to get to know the person and see what's on the inside, then one may be pleasantly suprised to find that the person is very different from what they imagined.

You can't teach an old dog new tricks

Meaning: It's challenging to teach a person something new, usually because that person has been doing what they do for so long that learning how to do it differently is difficult.

Origin: The idea of it being more difficult to teach things to an older dog has been around since at least the early 1500s. For example, in Fitzherbert's *Book of Husbandry*, 1534, it reads:

'He muste teche his dogge to barke whan he wolde haue hym, to ronne whan he wold haue hym, and to leue ronning whan he wolde haue gym; or els he is not a cunninge shepeherd. The dogge must lerne it, whan he is a whelpe, or els it wyl not be: for it is harde to make an olde dogge to stoupe.'

You're pulling my leg

Meaning: To tease someone or jokingly lie to them.

Origin: It actually has sinister origins, rooted in the criminal world of the 18th century. Street thieves would literally pull victims down by their leg in order to rob them more easily.

Your name is mud

Meaning: A person in trouble or worthless.

Origin: In the 1700s mud was a slang name for a fool or stupid person and was used throughout the 19th century by union workers. The word was used to refer to things that were polluting or worthless. It later was applied to people and was used as an insult implying that the person is worthless.

Z

Zero option

Meaning: The elimination of the Soviet SS20 missiles in return for abandoning the NATO Program.

Origin: A proposal made by President Reagan's administration on 19 November 1981.

Zero tolerance

Meaning: No tolerance for any anti-social or criminal behaviour.

Origin: William von Raab, who was the US Commissioner of Customs during the Reagan and first Bush administrations, carved the 'War on Drugs'. He did not tolerate drug crimes.

Zig-zag

Meaning: A series of short straight lines set at angles to one another and connected to form a continuous line. Often forming a regular pattern, but not necessarily so. This also denotes the action of moving along such a course.

Origin: This term seems to have come into English from Continental Europe—The Netherlands, France, or possibly Germany. The origin is unknown. The reduplication is suggestive of alternation, as with other phrases of that sort, e.g. tick-tock and see-saw.

www.ingramcontent.com/pod-product-compliance
Lightning Source LLC
Chambersburg PA
CBHW072251270326
41930CB00010B/2352